MW01067445

MICHAEL:

BECOME THE BEST

VERSION OF YOURSELF!

WHAT THEY'RE SAYING...
ABOUT *THE POWER OF A SYSTEM*

It is as if he is standing over your shoulder, advising you on how to set up your office to be successful. The book is very detailed and provides everything you need to build a successful practice.

I have been in practice a long time, and I like to think I am pretty bright, and I have a MBA but I have never been able to implement a good system. After reading his book, I realized that I did not know how. This book tells you how.

The book is going to make a difference—a big difference—in my practice.

—MICHAEL R. WADLER, ESQ., Harberg, Huvard, Jacobs & Wadler, LLP, Houston, Texas

---

How often do you get a "real" inside look at a successful lawyer's practice? This is basically his office manual in book form.

—BEN GLASS, ESQ., Ben Glass Law, Fairfax, Virginia

I absolutely love your book...I am outlining office procedures I need to implement. I keep looking to your System for guidance.

—PHILIP J. GIBBONS, Gibbons Law Group, Indianapolis, Indiana

I spent a good part of my vacation reading your book and it is amazing how much great information you covered. I will have my paralegals read it.

—STEVEN I. GOTTLIEB, ESQ., Moran & Gottlieb, Kingston, New York

WHAT OTHERS ARE SAYING ABOUT JOHN

John Fisher is, without a doubt, one of the brightest and most compassionate attorneys I have had the honor of not only knowing but working with on several major personal injury cases over the years. John is a brilliant trial attorney who truly cares about the people he represents and about the losses they suffered. His passion for justice is evident in everything that he becomes involved in.

—STEVEN I. GOTTLIEB, ESQ., Moran & Gottlieb, Kingston, New York

....

John is the preeminent attorney when it comes to medical malpractice cases. Recently I had the opportunity to observe John present a case to a jury focus group. I was very impressed with his command of the facts, use of modern technology, and persuasive style. I suspect that insurance companies would much rather settle than go to trial against John.

—SEAN DOOLAN, ESQ., Doolan & Platt, Windham, New York

....

From my first conversation with John Fisher, it was crystal clear that I was dealing with a top-tier attorney. John is very thorough, has an impressive level of knowledge about the medical profession, and takes the time and care necessary to make his clients comfortable and informed. I feel secure having John Fisher handling a matter very personal to me. He is the attorney attorneys hire and that is the highest endorsement of all! I am fortunate to be working with this consummate professional.

—ANNA MATULA-EVANS, ESQ., Poughkeepsie, New York

....

I have worked closely with Mr. Fisher and have found him to be one of the most conscientious, skilled, and committed lawyers I have known during my career. Both his work product and his character are exemplary.

—MARK GREENBERG, ESQ., Greenberg & Greenberg, Hudson, New York

----

A little over a year ago I referred a very difficult personal injury case to John Henry Fisher. The case had a number of potential pitfalls and complications. Mr. Fisher, along with his staff, provided nothing short of top-notch legal services in connection with the matter. Mr. Fisher provided personal service with amazing attention to all the details of the case.

The matter was resolved long before one could have reasonably expected resolution and the final settlement was truly magnificent based upon the complex facts.

I have been practicing law for about 20 years and have dealt with many different attorneys over that time and I can say without hesitation that Mr. Fisher handled this litigation as the consummate professional. I was privileged to work with Mr. Fisher on this matter and I can only hope that I can continue to work with him and his firm in the future.

—ANDREW M. COHEN, ESQ., Garden City, New York

Working in the professional field myself, I found it very comforting and reassuring to have John Fisher on my side. His extensive knowledge and attentiveness to my case continued to reaffirm that I had made the right choice in selecting him to represent me. John was very diligent, honest, hard-working and kept me in the loop every step of the way!

I have made referrals to him already, and will continue to do so.

I cannot express enough my level of gratitude for the wonderful job John has done, and the compassion and understanding that he portrayed. John, along with the wonderful staff in his firm, will continue to be the number-one pick for me, and for persons that I need to make referrals to. Thank you again for all you did for me.

—LINDA D. FAKHOURY, ESQ., Poughkeepsie, New York

*When I asked to print Linda's review, she replied,

Feel free to include my name! I meant every word of it. You did an amazing job. I work in the field of law and have dealt with lawyers both personally and professionally, but your work surpassed them all. Honestly.

I know the client is in good hands with you. Likewise I know you are making sure there is an A case. That is why you are the go-to lawyer for me and many others no doubt.

—SKIP SIMPSON, ESQ., Frisco, Texas

*When I asked to print Skip's review, he replied,

John, please feel free to publish any comment you wish. I don't make those comments for any reason other than they are the truth. I only wish the public knew our profession has many fine hard working men and women who became lawyers because they wanted to help others.

John Fisher is by far the most honest and diligent lawyer I have ever met in the medical malpractice field. Even though a client was not obtained, John still was able to give a client peace of mind for his legal issue. John is truly one of a kind and his highly recommended for any medical malpractice claims.

—SHAHZAD DAR, ESQ., Suffern, New York

Hi John. I just wanted to congratulate you on a really big win [settlement of a pediatric malpractice case at trial]. You just worked so hard for so long on this case and just dealt with every obstacle as it came down the pike.

I have a great deal of respect for your craftsmanship and how you went about dealing with this rather difficult and complicated case. You deserve all the credit. It's very nice working with you and I hope we will be collaborating on future cases.

Enjoy your win and I hope you get a little breather now because I know this was an intense case.

—MARIA D. LIFRAK, PhD, Comprehensive Neuropsychological Services, Albany, New York

----

After a family tragedy, we were searching for an attorney who would provide us with an honest assessment of a potential medical malpractice suit. By way of Texas and Washington DC we were referred to Mr. Fisher by an attorney and a PhD in behavioral health who described him as an expert in cases involving mental health issues.

From my initial contact through e-mail and receipt of a legal opinion that included a review of the medical record by an expert, Mr. Fisher was able to provide the necessary guidance my family needed to make the next step decision in 10 days.

He gave us a gift. The gift was to not leave us languishing for weeks in our pain before receiving an answer. We are grateful for his honesty, integrity, diligence, and professionalism.

—MARLENE A. SCHILLINGER, Syracuse, New York

It has been such a pleasure to work with John Fisher. His profession-alism is unsurpassed and his was extremely knowledgeable about the issue that I had to address. He offered guidance and he spent a great deal of time just reviewing the information I sent him. His website and book were extremely informative and saved me hours and hours of research.

Mr. Fisher has integrity, he is dedicated to his work, and he truly cares about his clients. I would recommend him to anyone who needs a lawyer. He is an amazing find!

—GILDA FALSO, Syracuse, New York

Thank you very much for all your efforts and support of my parents. Your compassion and assistance to my mother and father is greatly appreciated and went beyond the call of duty. My mother told me so! As you can imagine this entire event has been difficult, at least now with your help the issue of future funding will be satisfied.

—JACK VAN DER POEL, Chief Executive Officer of Shoe Depot, Concord, North Carolina

----

If you need the very best medical malpractice attorney for you or yours, then Mr. John Henry Fisher is the attorney I highly recommend. He is a brilliant very on-top-of-his-field guy, who goes after his clients cases with gusto like I've never seen.

I'm from Missouri, the "Show Me" state, and he did just that: he went right at the heart of the matter and indeed showed me that he is the best at what he does. Thank you, John H. Fisher, for every-thing. My hat will forever be off to you, sir.

—EDWARD SWENSON, Springfield, Missouri

This amazing man is far more than attorney. We met with John to see if there was merit for a malpractice case regarding a delay in diagnosis. John knows what he's talking about.

Complete respect for him being so direct. Many attorneys want you drooling out of their hand. John is reviewing my husband's medical records and promised us nothing.

The fact of the sincerity and expeditious review of this matter speaks volumes. Contacted by phone in the a.m. and seen later that evening just shows what you get.

—SARAH MILLER, Bennington, Vermont

I wanted to say "Thank you" for the way you handled my parents' case. You know your business well and you perform it well. Throughout this whole experience we always felt you handled my parents' needs and questions with respect, compassion, and professionalism.

—RAINA JOSBERGER, Coxsackie, New York

Very amazing and informative blog. Thanks for creating such a wonderful website [www.protectingpatientrights.com]. This website was not only knowledgeable but also very stimulating also. Thanks for sharing.

—THE WYNN GROUP, Dublin, Georgia

If you want to read more about John,
go to **www.avvo.com** and search "John Fisher Lawyer"
for reviews of John's work.

The Power of a
SYSTEM

The Power of a SYSTEM

How to Build the Injury Law
Practice of Your Dreams

John H. Fisher

Published by Advantage, Charleston, South Carolina.
Member of Advantage Media Group.

ADVANTAGE is a registered trademark and the Advantage colophon is a trademark of Advantage Media Group, Inc.

Printed in the United States of America.

ISBN: 978-1-59932-421-0
LCCN: 2013946956

This publication is designed to provide accurate and authoritative information in regard to the subject matter covered. It is sold with the understanding that the publisher is not engaged in rendering legal, accounting, or other professional services. If legal advice or other expert assistance is required, the services of a competent professional person should be sought.

Advantage Media Group is proud to be a part of the Tree Neutral® program. Tree Neutral offsets the number of trees consumed in the production and printing of this book by taking proactive steps such as planting trees in direct proportion to the number of trees used to print books. To learn more about Tree Neutral, please visit **www.treeneutral.com**. To learn more about Advantage's commitment to being a responsible steward of the environment, please visit **www.advantagefamily.com/green**

Advantage Media Group is a publisher of business, self-improvement, and professional development books and online learning. We help entrepreneurs, business leaders, and professionals share their Stories, Passion, and Knowledge to help others Learn & Grow. Do you have a manuscript or book idea that you would like us to consider for publishing? Please visit **advantagefamily.com** or call **1.866.775.1696**.

For making this book possible:
John K. Powers, Esq. and Daniel R. Santola, Esq.

"It is the system, not only the people, that will differentiate your business from everyone else's."

—Michael E. Gerber, *The E-Myth Revisited*

CONTENTS

Part 3   THE ENTREPRENEUR – 247

FOREWORD

THIS IS THE BOOK I WISH I HAD READ before I started my own practice.

A lot of lawyers start a law practice because, having worked for someone else, they come to the conclusion that "I'm a good lawyer. How hard could it be to start my own firm?" Maybe that's how you got started or maybe you picked up this book because you want to start your own firm.

Either way, I want to congratulate you. I was one of those lawyers who had done pretty well while working for someone else. Tried good cases. Got good verdicts and settlements. Really, how hard could starting my own practice be?

About a year into my practice I said to myself, "I really wish there was a step-by-step manual for all of the things I really needed to be good at to run a profitable practice." Sure, I could to go to CLEs on cross-examination or voir dire, and I did know how to give killer closing arguments, but I didn't have a clue about managing clients and employees. Systems? None. Good marketing ideas? I copied whatever everyone else was doing and that didn't turn out really well. Goal setting and business measurements? Didn't teach us that in law school!

I've known John Fisher for several years, and I've been looking over his shoulder a bit as he developed his own systems for running a profitable firm and then began sharing what he knew with other lawyers. I cheered for him when he started his own firm and I was thrilled to read an advance copy of this book *The Power of a System: How to Build the Injury Law Practice of Your Dreams.*

Though you may not agree with everything in the book, I can tell you that it will provoke your own thinking about (1) what your perfect law firm looks like, (2) who that perfect client is who will support the growth of your firm, (3) how to market to that perfect client, (4) how to manage that case from start to finish, and (5) how to build a superstar team around you so that you can devote your time to what you do best: adding value to your client's case through great lawyering.

Sadly, many lawyers give little to no thought to anything except "the lawyering" until it's too late. Though they are good lawyers, they lead lives of misery because the practice lacks sound business fundamentals.

Don't be *that* lawyer. John Fisher wants you to enjoy the practice of law more by showing you exactly what you need to do to get those vital business systems in place.

This is the book I wish I had read when I went out on my own in 1995. It would have eliminated a lot of pain.

Ben Glass, Fairfax, VA
Ben Glass Law
Great Legal Marketing

INTRODUCTION

MY DAY OF RECKONING had finally arrived … and I was scared to death.

At first it seemed like just another day at work. After 19 years of practice as a litigation lawyer, there was nothing that made this day unlike any other, so commonplace, in fact, that I don't recall what I did that morning other than sit at my desk and do some sort of work.

But then a bomb dropped.

The firm's founding partners wanted to see me. This can't be good, I thought. If the top partners at the firm wanted to see me, they would just come to my office or send me an e-mail. But this was different, and I knew it.

The scary news was just as I expected. With a somber and serious expression on his face, the senior partner conveyed the frightening news, "John, it's time we part ways." Thoughts raced through my mind, "How will I tell my wife that I no longer have a job—for the first time in 19 years? How will I pay the bills next month? "

Life as a partner at a law firm did not quite have the job security that a young lawyer fresh out of law school might think. Now, I was being shown the door, and for the first time in my career, I was on my own with no safety nets or job security. The time had arrived to make a living on my own with no secretary or paralegal, no office, and no computers.

But the problem facing me was far more serious. For just about my entire career as a lawyer, I had been the guy *doing the work*, which for the most part involved handling the nuts and bolts of a lawsuit ranging from depositions, motions, discovery responses, and trial. For me, this was just fun, and I never really wanted to do anything else.

What They Don't Teach You in Law School

Even as a seasoned trial lawyer, sweat drenched the top of my back when I got the scary news. Now, for the first time in my career, I was facing the task of running my own law firm. No problem for this seasoned trial lawyer, right?

Yes, I had a problem. You see, they never taught me how to run my own law firm in law school. Yes, you leave law school well versed in torts, contracts, and constitutional law, but there is not even a single hour of instruction on managing and operating your own law firm. Like virtually all lawyers practicing as associates or even most partners, I did not have the slightest clue how to manage and run my own firm. I was woefully unprepared for the reality that was about to hit.

This is where my vision started.

For me, reality was harsh. Running around from one task to the next like a chicken with its head cut off, it quickly became clear I needed a plan. But more than just a plan, I needed a system for managing and operating a law firm. I needed systems for every aspect of my firm from the financial payroll and goals to minutiae such as answering the phones. So, I started writing and writing. I started building a collection of every system that I either had or should have for my law firm.

When a new system entered my mind, I wrote more, but not only systems for the daily technical aspects of running a law firm. I set out to create systems for strategic planning, bonus-based compensation, and goal setting on a daily, quarterly, and yearly basis, and I created one "big audacious goal" for my personal future.

A Confession from Yours Truly

In hindsight there's little doubt I've learned much more from my mistakes than successes. That's why I give an explanatory notation ("Why it's done this way") for the systems for running a law firm. I've learned how to run a law firm … and *what not to do* in running a firm.

Yes, I confess that I've made tons of mistakes. And each mistake has been a learning opportunity that I've used to fine-tune the systems for running a law firm. I hope you benefit from my mistakes and the lessons I've learned from them, so you don't repeat the same mistakes.

"Double your rate of failure … You're thinking of failure as the enemy of success. But it isn't at all … So go ahead and make mistakes. Make all you can. Because, remember, that's where you'll find success. On the other side of failure."

—Thomas J. Watson Sr., founder of IBM

The founder of IBM's formula for success is simple: *double your rate of failure*. If you fail repeatedly, you will be the subject of ridicule and scorn from your peers—and on the road to success.

A Big Warning

One word of caution before we begin: just having systems in place for your law firm will accomplish nothing. *You have to implement the systems!*

If you simply read this book and don't take steps to implement these principles, you are wasting your time. But, I know, Rome wasn't created in a day, and you can't create the law firm of your dreams in a single afternoon. Rather, I encourage you to take one small step to implement these principles every day.

Taking control of your law firm's future is only a few daily actions away. With one small baby step after the next, you will be slowly but surely on your way to create a law firm that is the rival of your peers. So, before going any further, I need one commitment from you. Don't keep reading until you commit, out loud, to having one daily goal.

Yes, that's right: only one goal. And it's okay if your goal is simple and takes little time. If you take one daily goal and take action to implement the goal every day, you will be well on your way to the law firm of your dreams.

A Word of Explanation

Throughout this book I refer to the civil case management software Trialworks. In my humble view, Trialworks is the best civil case management software on the market today, but it's not the only one, and you may likely have different software for your firm. When I use Trialworks in this book, you will know that I am referring to a civil case management software program.

Some parts of this book incorporate strategies and procedures that at times specifically relate to New York law. If you do not practice law in New York, I hope you can use the concepts as they apply in your state or country.

The three parts of this book, The Technician, The Manager, and The Entrepreneur, are based upon Michael E. Gerber's classic book, *The E-Myth Revisited*, which sets forth three general rules for business owners in any industry. Whether you realize it or not, most of your time is spent "in your business" doing the technical lawyer work. And hey, the work has to get done. But the mindset change for you is to begin setting aside time every day, preferably hours that are scheduled just like a meeting with a client or court conference, to think about strategies for the growth of your law firm through delegation, outsourcing, and marketing. Give yourself permission today to begin spending time working *on* your business (strategic thinking) instead of only spending time *in* your business (the technical work).

This book leaves no stone unturned in providing systems for all three roles that you have as the owner of your law firm, the technician, the manager, and the entrepreneur. You have my explicit permission to copy the systems and rules in this book for your law firm and incorporate as much (or as little) of the rules in your office manual. Hey, I've learned from plenty of mistakes during 21 years of practice and I want to give you the benefit of my mistakes (what not to do) so you don't have to repeat them.

THE FIRST (AND MOST IMPORTANT) STEP TO CREATING THE LAW PRACTICE OF YOUR DREAMS

WHENEVER YOU ASK your lawyer friends how they're doing, you always get the same answer. The answer is so matter-of-fact that you could answer the question before you're finished asking: "I am so busy you wouldn't believe it." It seems that lawyers are just like everyone: extremely busy. You run around doing lawyer stuff that you never seem to have time to sit down and just think, *"Why am I doing this?"*

But if you never ask "WHY" you are doing what you do, you will be doomed to the life of the lab rat running endlessly on a flywheel. Unless you know why you are doing the "lawyer work," you will never have a life of purpose and meaning.

To create a life of purpose and meaning, you must first take the time to sit down and think of the vision for your career (and it wouldn't hurt to think of the vision for your life too while you're at it). I know what you're thinking: I have no time for this "vision stuff," I've got work to do. And it's completely okay if you want to keep doing things like every other lawyer in your town (I'm not passing judgment), but if you do what everyone else is doing, you will be just like them: average.

> **"Until you're clear where you're going, it's hard to get there."**
>
> —CLATE MASK, CEO & FOUNDER OF INFUSIONSOFT

Vision provides clarity, alignment and inspiration for your employees and gives a higher purpose to your staff than just earning money. In other words, it's important that you exist and do what you do. A law firm without vision is like a boat without a rudder—there is nothing guiding you or your employees. You may be moving, but you're just floating aimlessly without a specific destination. Once you get the vision clear, it acts as a magnet for the type of talent in alignment with your vision. You can then hire, train and fire based on your vision.

Vision instills clarity and confidence from chaos and confusion

Setting the vision for your law firm requires three things: PURPOSE, VALUES and MISSION. There is no more important thing you can do for your career that to establish the purpose, values and mission for your law practice. So if you're still with me, let's get started with your purpose.

> **"It is impossible to have a great life unless it's a meaningful life."**
>
> —JIM COLLINS, *Good to Great*

PURPOSE: WHAT YOU STAND FOR AND WHY YOU EXIST

The PURPOSE for your law career is why you exist and is the north-star that always guides everything that you do. Your purpose is what gets you out of bed in the morning and gets you excited to go to work every day. Your purpose never changes, has no duration and lasts your entire career.

To find your purpose, you need to ask, "What do I stand for?" And remember, your employees want to have a purpose; salary only motivates up to a certain point. Get your employees to understand why you're in business.

> ### "Organizations should put more effort into identifying their purpose."
>
> —JIM COLLINS, *Built to Last*

But it's not easy figuring out exactly what you stand for and why you do what you do—it may take you days to figure out why you exist. The purpose for our law firm started as, *"Providing Clear Answers to Complex Medical Malpractice Questions"* and then I thought, "But why do we do that? Is this really the ultimate reason we practice law?" No!

Our purpose evolved to, *"Raising the Standard of Care for All Patients."* Yuck! Way too technical and not exactly something that gets you out of bed on cold, dark mornings. This sounds more like a hospital's slogan than the purpose for our plaintiffs' medical malprac-tice firm. So we kept pushing the envelope to define why we exist.

When pushed harder to reflect on our "WHY," there was only one thing that we kept coming back to, *"Stopping Medical Injustice."* Bingo! Our purpose, "Stopping Medical Injustice," is simple, clear and will remain our purpose for as long we're open for business. This is "why" we exist as a law firm.

Do you have a big, bold purpose for your law firm? If not, it's never too late to create your purpose (and put you ahead of 99% of everyone else). You will never be a great law firm without identifying your purpose and communicating it with your staff.

VALUES: CORE PRINCIPLES THAT GUIDE EVERYTHING YOU DO

Your VALUES consist of 5-10 principles that you live by and guide all of the work you do. The duration of your values is forever. Your core values are essential and enduring tenets that will guide you and your team as long as you exist.

What are your core values? Just by way of example, our core values are:

- We limit our practice to catastrophic injury law for injury victims.

- We do not accept cases that have questionable merit.

- We accept very few cases.

- We always put our clients' interests first.

- We treat our clients like family.

- We do the right thing.

- We do what we say we'll do.

- We practice open, real communication.

- We check our egos at the door.

- We invest in continuous improvement.

These are the core values that will guide our law firm forever. But everyone is different. So you should begin thinking of the core values that will guide you and your law firm as long as you exist.

MISSION: YOUR "BIG, HAIRY, AUDACIOUS GOAL"

The MISSION lasts 3 to 5 years and is specific enough that it can be checked off. This is your chance to inspire your people and is an opportunity to be bold ("Wow, that's a big deal!").

Do not make your vision to be a specific profit figure—your staff will not get excited about revenue numbers. You want your team to feel they are part of something much bigger than just another law firm. You are an elite law firm—not just a bunch of lawyers trying to scratch together a living. But to get to this special place, you must have a well-defined mission that is communicated to your team.

> *"To defy the odds, to take on big hairy challenges—especially if rooted in ideology—does much to make people feel that they belong to something special, elite, different, better."*
>
> —JIM COLLINS, *Built to Last*

You should not define your mission by what others are doing. This is a recipe for mediocrity. Doing what everyone else is doing is by definition average. You need a mission that is unique, bold and gives your team a higher sense of purpose than simply making money.

What is your Economic Engine?

In Jim Collins's classic book, *Good to Great*, he explains that every great business must define its "economic engine." Your economic engine is the economic denominator that makes you successful; it is your most profitable and sustainable business model. You should ask, "What is the source of your best cases and highest return on investment?"

By way of example, our "economic engine" is referrals from other lawyers (just like you). Since we don't do mass marketing, our best cases are generated by new cases referred by lawyers. It's simple— we don't stay in business without your referrals. Now that it's clear that our economic engine is lawyer referrals, our mission statement is simple:

> "To be the #1 law firm for lawyers referring medical
> malpractice cases in Upstate New York."

The question to ask is, "What you is your economic engine?" What makes you successful and is the most lucrative and profitable thing you do? Once you have this answer, you know what your "economic engine" is.

What is your Mission?

But it's not enough to just have a mission statement, you should set big, bold goals that are consistent with your mission. We call these annual goals our "base camps," i.e., annual goals that are specific and measurable that will take us to our ultimate goal at the peak of the mountain.

Here's how we bring our mission statement into alignment with our goals. As of October 19, 2013, we had 124 "Referral Partners." A "referral partner" is an attorney, paralegal or someone in the legal field (i.e., Executive Director of the Bar Association), who has referred a case to our law firm in the last five years. Our current MISSION is to increase the number of Referral Partners to 500 by October 19, 2017 (yes, our Mission is bold and a big stretch for us).

At every one-year interval, we have specific goals (called the "Base Camp") that we must meet in order to reach the top of the mountain.

Base Camp #1: 2013 = 124 Referral Partners;

Base Camp #2: 2014 = 185 Referral Partners (+61);

Base Camp #3: 2015 = 265 Referral Partners (+80);

Base Camp #4: 2016 = 365 Referral Partners (+100); and

Base Camp #5: 2017 = 500 **Referral Partners** (+135)

You should post your numbers on a poster board or TV monitor and update them weekly. You communicate your mission to your team and update them on your progress in order to make them clear what you are trying to achieve.

It's not enough that you know your mission—your team should too and they should be constantly reminded of what you are seeking to do. Because let's face it, you'll never get to the top of the mountain without your team being on board and pulling in the same direction.

Hiring, training and firing to the Vision

The purpose, values and mission must be more than just a founder's statement. Once you draft your purpose, values and mission, you're only 70% done. Your team members have to co-create your purpose, values and mission so you ask them to review them and make changes. The foundation for your law firm is a shared vision.

But it's not enough to just have a vision for your law practice—you must reinforce your culture at every turn: hiring, training and firing. All employees must memorize the purpose, values and mission of your law firm. Before you interview prospective employees, you ask them to memorize your purpose, values and mission of your law firm and at the interview, ask her, "Okay, tell us what are the purpose, values and mission?" Now you know if you've got a serious candidate for the job.

Ideally, you can use the physical space of your law office to reinforce the purpose, values and mission, i.e., posting your purpose, values and mission in your conference and copy rooms. But don't just stop with the physical office space, you can put your purpose on your letterhead, monthly newsletters and in the electronic signature of your emails. You want your purpose, values and mission to be everywhere so everyone knows what you stand for.

Does this sound hard? Well, it should and remember, "Life in a visionary company is not supposed to be easy." Jim Collins, *Built to Last*.

Part 1
THE TECHNICIAN

*"The value of your practice
is in your systems."*

—Michael E. Gerber, *The E-Myth Attorney*

1

THE OFFICE RULES

"In battlefield conditions it is most useful for everyone to have been brought up on and conditioned to perform within absolutely rigid standards. It is my contention that the very same thing is true in business."

—DAN KENNEDY, *No B.S. Ruthless Management of People & Profits*

YOUR LAW PRACTICE IS THRIVING, you have all the clients you could want, and the money is flowing. Suddenly, everything changes. A drunk driver crashes into your car at an intersection, and you suffer a traumatic brain injury, which puts you in a coma for six months.

So, what happens to your law practice? I'm sure you've already got that answer. Chaos! Your staff is completely lost at first and look for direction. Even worse, your clients are wondering whether they have to switch lawyers, and you are suddenly on the verge of losing the biggest cases of your career. Your law practice totters on the brink of ruin. By the time you recover from your injuries, it may be too late.

Can this nightmare scenario happen to you? Let's hope not. But you have to prepare for the worst.

Now, let's put a prettier ending in place for this nightmare. Instead of running out like chickens with their heads off, your secretaries, paralegals, and receptionist know exactly what to do because you have systems in place for exactly this situation.

Each staff member in your office has a "position contract" (I'll explain later) that thoroughly and specifically identifies what they are supposed to do. No one is asking, "What do I do now?" The position contract tells them what they should do and your law practice purrs like a finely tuned race car.

You get the picture? Everyone knows what to do and what is expected of them in your law practice. You emerge from the coma with the knowledge that your law practice still exists and cases have been settled while you were on your death bed. You decide to take a long rehabilitation and six months later, after your complete recovery, your law practice is still making money.

This is the benefit to you of having systems in place in your law practice.

Okay, so here is the assignment to do right now. Imagine what your law practice would be like (even whether it would still exist) if you lapsed into a coma for the next six months. My guess is that you refuse to think about it, you've never thought about it, and you're not going to think about it. I don't blame you; it's not a pretty picture.

But here's the good news. There is a solution that will help you with your law practice right now. You must develop operational rules that enable your employees to deal with problems themselves instead of calling for your help. With this training manual, you can train new employees almost instantly. If a key employee leaves your law firm, you can have the new employee produce a result that is identical to what the person who just left would have produced.

You don't have to lapse into a coma for this system to work. In fact, the system will begin working for you and giving you results, now.

So, what are you waiting for? Let's get started with the basics.

My Goal

Whenever I hire a new secretary and a mistake is made, I get the same response, "You didn't tell me to do it that way." I wrote this book so you will know exactly what is expected of you. There will be no confusion about what is expected of you or what your duties are.

Your job is not to create more work for me. Your job is to eliminate the endless interruptions to my productive work time, so I can focus my time and energy on the 20 percent of cases that will make the most money for us.

This book describes the work that you are accountable for, and a list of the standards by which your results are to be evaluated. The position contract that you will sign is a contract between you and me that summarizes the rules of your position. By signing the position contract, you agree to fulfill those responsibilities.

What is the best way to prepare for your job with me? You should read this book as often as possible and then come ready to work.

This means, for example, that you should never ask me for a "status report" on a case. If you want to get the status of a case, you should check the Notes tab in Trialworks, where I enter updates of almost every phone conversation, court appearance, and to-do jobs. If you ask me to give you the "status" on a case, you are creating more work for me, and I don't like that.

My Worldview

My goal is to focus on the work that *only I can do* and have you do everything else. For instance, I would never ask you to handle a malpractice trial or deposition because that's my job, and you are not licensed to practice law. There are certain things that only I can do, and those are the only things I should be doing.

Besides malpractice depositions and trials, there's not a lot more that only I can do. I like to prepare expert responses and the allegations of negligence in the bill of particulars, but that's only because I like doing those things.

Your job is to do everything else. This includes getting medical records, communicating with clients, preparing discovery responses, scheduling depositions, and making sure deadlines are met.

YOU HAVE THE POWER TO MAKE DECISIONS WITHOUT ME:
You have authority to act without interrupting me. Do not ask me, "Should the expert witness fly into LaGuardia or JFK Airport?" I don't care. I trust you to make the right decision.

DON'T ASK ME FOR PERMISSION:
Do what you think is right and we'll make adjustments as we go along. You are not a problem reporter. You are a problem solver. You should never ask me a question if you can get the answer without asking me. *I encourage you to take more risks!*

Use your judgment and make your best decision. This is my official written permission for you to fix all problems without contacting me. I am empowering you to make decisions for me without asking for my permission, and you have my permission to make mistakes.

I don't want my staff members looking over their shoulders every time they make a decision. You were hired for a good reason: you are smart and highly skilled. Now, I expect you will use those skills. That's why I want you to make decisions without asking for my permission. I want you to be self-sufficient.

I don't want you to ask questions throughout the work day. I do not need the constant interruptions. If you have questions that must be addressed by me, and you cannot solve them on your own, write them down and set up a time to speak with me. If you can get your written questions to me in advance, I will set up a time to speak with you between 4 p.m. and 5 p.m.

If you can solve a question without asking me, do not bother me with it.

E-mail Use

E-mails are for the most part a waste of my time so I do my best to avoid them completely. I only check e-mail twice a day, once at noon and again at 4 p.m. I never check my e-mail first thing in the morning, so don't expect a response.

If I respond to each e-mail I get, I would get no work done. And it's always tempting to respond to e-mails as a thoughtless interruption of work. I just avoid e-mails completely with the exception of two times a day. Even if I read your e-mail, there is a strong chance I won't respond to it, so this is not a great way to get my attention.

Internet Use

The Internet is a great way to avoid doing work. Let's face it, the Internet is the greatest temptation. It's so easy to rationalize that you will only spend a few minutes on Facebook checking out what your sister did last weekend. *There should be no web surfing at work.*

We monitor Internet use at our office: If you surf the World Wide Web, we will know when you are doing it, what websites you are going to, and how long you spend on the Internet. So don't think for a minute that we don't know you are on the Internet.

The following is our firm's policy concerning the use of email and the internet. While all aspects of the policy are of equal importance, you should pay special attention to items numbered 2 and 3. The firm's computer system permanently records every email that is sent or received and every website that is accessed from the firm's computers. Copies of this information are backed-up and kept at a secure off-site location.

With regard to website access, the system records the name of the person who visited each website, the date and time the website was accessed, and the length of time the person visited the website.

1. All systems and equipment are the property of our law firm and are to be used only for business purposes;

2. You should not have any expectation of privacy when using our systems and equipment;

3. All systems and equipment will be monitored and employee use of the systems and equipment constitutes consent to monitoring;

4. Email for personal purposes is prohibited;

5. Use of the internet for personal purposes is prohibited;

6. All information and data stored on the systems or equipment is confidential and is the exclusive property of our law firm;

7. No information or data stored on the systems or equipment shall be used, copied or transferred, by any means, for any reason that is not directly related to the business purposes of our law firm.

Please sign this policy to acknowledge that you are fully aware of our law firm's policies regarding the use of email and the internet.

Cell-Phone Use

You should never text or make calls on your cell phone unless you have a family emergency. A family emergency would be your son just had an accident and is en route to the emergency room.

Dress Code

You should not dress like a slob. You should never wear jeans, T-shirts, or sneakers. If you have nose rings, remove them. You should be dressed conservatively as though you plan to attend a funeral.

You will often be asked to come to court to meet witnesses or deliver exhibits during a trial. If you appear at the trial, you don't want to look as if you just got out of bed. It is difficult to predict when you may be called to assist at the courthouse, so the best bet is to dress professionally all the time.

No-Gossip Rule

We have a no-gossip rule. If you've got the urge to gossip, trouble is heading your way. If you've got a complaint about a coworker, everything stays inhouse. You should never bring the gossip or work issues outside the office.

Personal Errands and Timeliness

Your job is to make my job and my life easier. If I ask you to pick up lunch for me, don't question why. As the Nike commercial says, "Just do it."

It won't happen often, but when I have a trial, you may be asked to do personal errands such as bringing lunch to my expert witness or driving the witness from my office to court. That is part of your job.

You are expected to be on time. If you start work at 9 a.m., you should be at your desk and ready to work with your computer on at

9 a.m. If your work day ends at 5 p.m., you shouldn't begin packing up your things at 4:55 p.m. You should be working at your desk until 5 p.m. sharp.

Personal Errands at Work

You should never do personal errands at work—period! During your work hours at the office, you should not be paying your bills, getting an oil change for your car, or making day-care arrangements for your kids.

Your personal errands should be done in your *free* time, not when you are supposed to be working. Unless you have a medical emergency with your family, you should never do personal errands during work hours.

If it is completely unavoidable, you must ask for permission from me to do a personal errand during work hours. You do not have my permission to do personal errands until you ask by e-mail and I reply, "Okay." Otherwise, the answer is no.

Completing Assignments

If I tell you that a work assignment must be completed before the end of the day, you should not leave work that day without completing the assignment. If you cannot complete the assignment by the end of the day, you must ask for my permission to do the work the following day.

Document Preparation

You should prepare all documents in Microsoft Word 2007 or 2010. *I do not use Microsoft Word Perfect* because it is outdated and barely used. You should not create any documents in Microsoft Word Perfect.

You should create documents using the Arial font, size 12. If you create documents in another font or size, I will have to convert them and that's a waste of my time.

You should double space all documents. The only time you should single space is for a block quotation within a document.

Your Vacations

You should not schedule a vacation the week before a trial. The week before a trial is the time when I need you the most.

You should not call in sick on a day that falls on the week before a trial. If you are sick enough to call in sick on the week before a trial, you better be in a hospital.

My Vacations

If I am away on vacation, you should not call me unless it truly is an emergency. I do not check my e-mail or text messages during vacation because I do not want to be interrupted. You get the picture.

Profanity in the Office

You should never use profanity in the office. But if you are tempted and you just can't resist, you should leave the building and go somewhere no one will hear you before you shout profanities at the top of your lungs. You are part of a world class business and profanities have no place in our business.

When I Am Out of the Office

When I am out of the office and clients call for me, the receptionist will forward the phone calls to you. You should answer our clients' questions and address their concerns. Do your best to answer our clients' questions so I do not have to call them.

You should keep me informed about your contact with our clients by sending me an e-mail briefly describing the situation, for example, "Mr. Jones requested copies of his bill of particulars and I gave them to him."

IME

Never use the word IME: A physical examination of our client done at the request of the defense lawyer should never be called an IME. I never want to hear or see those words. You should always call the defense examination by its correct name, "defense medical examination," or DME.

Even if the judge refers to the defense medical exam as an IME, you should never use that word or include such a term in a proposed scheduling order.

Why it's done this way: The abbreviation IME portrays the defense examination as an independent exam, when in fact it is never independent. I do not accept this bogus jargon and neither should you.

John's Philosophy about New Cases Unrelated to Personal Injury

If prospective clients call with types of case that I don't handle—for example, a personal bankruptcy—you should not tell them that I cannot handle their case. You should explain to the prospective clients that you will find the right lawyer for their case. You should then ask me for the name of a lawyers to whom you can refer the prospective clients.

Why it's done this way: The only reason I get referrals from other lawyers is that I refer cases to them. The best thing you can do to nurture referral relationships with other lawyers is to send them new cases, even if there is no referral fee that I can get. Lawyers love referrals from me and it is your job to help me send referrals to other lawyers.

Fax Cover Sheets

You should not handwrite the transmittal sheet for faxes. You should always type the fax transmittal sheet on the form in our network. A handwritten fax transmittal sheet looks unprofessional.

Criminal Background Checks of New Clients

When I accept a new case (this means I decide to file a lawsuit), you should send a written request via facsimile to the court administration office for a criminal background check on our client. You should never assume our client has been honest about his past. In fact, you should assume our clients will lie to you.

You should always confirm with the court administration office that our clients do not have a criminal background. This is not a discretionary decision on your part; you should do a criminal background search for all of our clients, including our church-going, elderly clients.

Social Media Background Check of New Clients

After I accept a new client's case and file a lawsuit, you should check our client's social media profiles on Facebook, Twitter, and so on, for inappropriate content (e.g., a profile photograph of our client pointing a gun into his mouth) and send me an e-mail if you find any embarrassing content.

Totally Swamped with Work?

If you are up to your neck in work and don't know what to do, I have an answer: outsource. That's right. There's nothing wrong with outsourcing the mundane, data entry projects to persons outside our law firm.

I use Elance.com to outsource data entry projects. There is a bevy of workers across the globe just waiting to do your work for very small fees. Not only do I approve outsourcing your work, I applaud you for delegating the menial, data-entry projects that should not be consuming your time.

You have my absolute permission and authority to outsource work. If outsourcing will make you more efficient, there is no need for you to ask my permission. I have a number of secretaries and paralegals whom I've hired through Elance.com, and I will give you their contact information as soon as you want to begin outsourcing.

Here's how it works: On Monday afternoon, you outsource a project to a company in India—for example, Your Man in India (YMII) or Brickwork—and on Tuesday morning when you return to the office, voilà! Your work is done and ready for your review in your e-mail box. This is, in essence, the 24-hour law office and it's truly a thing of beauty. Instead of the typical eight-hour workday for 99 percent of law firms, *we become a 24-hour working machine*. All it takes is one taste of outsourcing and you will be sold.

If you ever think, "I have way more work than I can get done," you shouldn't ask me what to do. You've got my answer: outsource.

When All Else Fails

Here's a basic office rule: if your door is closed, I will not open your door or knock. You will be left alone in complete silence.

When the door to your office is closed, that means you want no interruptions at all and need complete quiet to get your work done. You have my permission to close your door when you want to. I would far rather you be productive than you worry about hurting my feelings.

And by the way, if you need a day or two to get caught up with your work, just send me an e-mail stating, "No interruptions please for two days" and voila! You just got two days of uninterrupted work time.

Why it's done this way: I understand that you need peace and quiet to get your work done. So, don't be bashful; close your door and I will leave you alone to get your work done. This is perfectly acceptable with me.

E-mails

TRANSFERRING ALL E-MAILS TO TRIALWORKS

All e-mails should be created and sent through Trialworks, so there is a record of the e-mails applicable to each case. You should not send e-mails through Outlook.

If you or I receive an e-mail through Outlook, you should *always* transfer the e-mail from Outlook to the E-mail tab in Trialworks. In the upper corner of Outlook, you right-click the tab for Trialworks, identify the case where you will transfer the e-mail and voilà, the e-mail is transferred from Outlook to Trialworks.

Why it's done this way: When you go to the E-mail tab in Trialworks, you will be able to review a complete list of every e-mail applicable to the case. Just as letters and motions must be organized and placed under the appropriate tab in Trialworks, the same is true for e-mails.

RESPONDING TO E-MAILS

I will include your e-mail address on all e-mails that I receive and send. When an e-mail is received from a client or lawyer, you should respond to all that you can, and send me a copy of your responding e-mail. You should filter my e-mails so I do not have to respond to every e-mail I receive. Answering e-mail is a huge waste of my time.

If you can answer my e-mail for me, just respond without asking for my permission. You have my complete permission to respond to e-mails as you consider appropriate. Do not worry if you make a mistake. If you're not sure whether you should respond, just respond and keep me in the loop by sending a copy of your e-mail to me.

URGENT MATTERS

Do not use e-mail if you need an immediate response: You should not send me an e-mail if you need me to respond to an urgent e-mail. I don't check e-mail often and it is likely I will not even read your e-mail if you need a response urgently. Remember, I only check e-mail at noon and 4:00 p.m. every day.

Mail

WHAT YOU SHOULD DO WITH MAIL

You should not give me hard copies of mail. Incoming mail should be scanned by you into Trialworks and e-mailed to me as soon as you receive the mail. If you leave hard copies of mail in my office, they will be forever lost or ignored. So you should *never* leave hard copies of mail in my office.

Under no circumstances will it be acceptable to e-mail the incoming mail to me on a day after it is received.

Why it's done this way: If you e-mail my mail to me a few days after you received it, my mail may become outdated and stale. For example, on December 29 we receive a letter from defense counsel stating that a tractor trailer will be available for inspection on January 3. Instead of e-mailing the letter to me on December 29 (when you received it), you e-mail the letter to me on January 4. As a result, I missed a crucial opportunity to inspect the tractor trailer and our client's case will now be more difficult to prove. You get the picture.

JUNK MAIL AND SOLICITATIONS

I do not need to read junk mail. If I get a solicitation in the mail and you think it's junk that I don't need to see, throw it away without asking for my permission.

RESPONDING TO MAIL

You should review my mail. If you can answer my mail, answer it. You should respond to all of my mail that you can without bothering me. If you believe a letter should be addressed by me (e.g., a letter making a settlement offer), bring this letter to my attention by e-mail.

If you can respond to my mail, prepare the letter, sign it, and mail the letter with your signature. Your job is to make my life as easy as possible and that includes addressing as much of my mail as you can.

Phone Calls from Sales Reps

If sales reps call for me, ask them to state the reason for their call in a fax. I will only consider speaking with them if they follow this procedure. I will consider scheduling a phone call with sales reps only after I get their fax and I decide to schedule the phone call.

I will not accept unscheduled phone calls from sales reps.

Out-of-State Travel for Meetings

When I ask you to schedule out-of-state travel for me, there are three rules of thumb:

Rental Cars: I only rent cars from Enterprise. The economy or budget car is just fine. I don't need a fancy car to impress anyone. Even if another rental company has a lower fare, I still prefer Enterprise.

Air Travel: I prefer to fly on JetBlue. If you cannot book a flight on JetBlue, my second favorite is Southwest. I always prefer paying the extra $50 for the seats with extra legroom (called Economy

Comfort or something similar). I try to avoid every airline that's not named JetBlue or Southwest.

I hate layovers during air travel. Unless it is completely unavoidable, you should always reserve a direct flight from my home airport to the final destination.

Hotels: I prefer Hilton Hotels or any of their branch hotels. If there is no Hilton Hotel in the area where I am traveling, you can reserve a room at the hotel offering the lowest available daily rate.

My Closed-Door Policy

If the door to my office is closed, you should not knock or open my door unless it is an emergency. When my door is closed, this means I am busy working and *I do not want to be bothered*. An "emergency" means, "The statute of limitations will expire today if you don't file the summons and complaint" or "Are you available to drive me to the hospital? I'm about to have a baby."

You should limit your contact with me to specified times during the day—namely, between 4:00 p.m. and 5:00 p.m. I do not have an open-door policy.

Why it's done this way: It is impossible to get work done if I have a constant flow of interruptions. If you have something that is important, send me an e-mail and schedule a time to speak with me later in the day between 4:00 p.m. and 5:00 p.m.

Blocking Out Time in the Calendar

If I block out time in the calendar—for example, 9:00 a.m. to 11:00 a.m. is blocked out in Microsoft Outlook—that means I am busy working on a specific project and I will not accept any interruptions. This means you should not bother me.

Scheduling Appointments in Microsoft Outlook

You are responsible for scheduling all of my appointments.

If the time slot is not blocked off in Microsoft Outlook—for example, the time slot between 2:30 p.m. and 3:30 p.m. has no appointments—I am available, and you can schedule an appointment for me. You should not ask for my permission to schedule an appointment. If the time slot is open in Microsoft Outlook, I am available and you can schedule an appointment without asking for my permission.

You should not simply block out time in Microsoft Outlook for my appointments. Rather, you should state the specific time of the appointment in Outlook. You should schedule my appointments in Microsoft Outlook as follows: "JHF—court conference at 9:30 a.m. (name of client)."

You should be as specific as possible when scheduling appointments in Microsoft Outlook. For example, if a new client requests a 30-minute phone appointment to discuss questions about the retainer agreement, you should enter the appointment in Microsoft Calendar as, "JHF—phone appointment with new client, Mr. Jones, to discuss his questions about the retainer agreement."

Why it's done this way: If you block out sixty minutes in Microsoft Outlook for my appointment—for example, you block out sixty minutes between 9:30 a.m. and 10:30 a.m.—I will be forced to guess whether my court conference is at 9:30 a.m., 10:00 a.m., or 10:30 a.m. I hate guessing. It is far better for you to specify the exact time of my appointment in Microsoft Outlook. That removes the guesswork and makes it easy for me to know the time of my appointment.

Completion of Assignments

You should not assume I know that you are doing your job. When you complete a job assignment (e.g., discovery responses and demands), you should send me an e-mail to let me know the work has been completed and is ready for my review. For example, your e-mail should read, "Finalized all discovery responses and demands in Mrs. Jones's case. They are ready for your review." Another example would be, "Today, I mailed written requests for all of our client's medical records."

Why it's done this way: Your e-mails will let me know that a task has been completed and can be crossed off my to-do list. Otherwise, I will have to review the file to make sure you are doing your job and that's not a good use of my time.

2

CLIENT COMMUNICATION

"A very visible secret about companies that really prosper is that they have clearly understood covenants with their customers."

—DAN KENNEDY, *No B.S. Ruthless Management of People & Profits*

ON THE FIRST DAY clients arrive to meet with us, they should be handed our "shock-and-awe" package for new clients. The shock-and-awe is a welcome package for new clients that sets the standards and rules between our clients and our law firm and helps educate clients about the procedures to expect in their lawsuit.

The shock-and-awe package is intended to accomplish exactly what it's called, namely, showing up like no one else. The shock-and-awe package consists of the following items:

- My book *The Seven Deadly Mistakes of Malpractice Victims*. The books should be signed by me and personalized for each client, for example, "Dear Mary";

- Audio CDs: "How to Win a Lawsuit against Your Doctor," "The Top Three Mistakes Made by Injury Victims When Hiring an Injury Lawyer," and "The Three Little Secrets Your Injury Lawyer Will Never Tell You";

- Binder of office policies, including: "The Three Rules of Communication," "Your Eight Basic Rights: How to Make Sure Your Injury Lawyer Is Doing His Job," and "Rules for Protecting Your Privacy and Confidentiality Rights."

The Three Rules of Communication

"The Three Rules of Communication" document explains our communication policies with new clients:

- From day one, it is important that our new clients understand that (1) I do not take unscheduled phone calls (yes, the new clients must schedule a time to speak or meet with me); (2) I do not accept "walk-in" appointments. If new clients just show up and expect to meet with me, they will be told to schedule an appointment (if I am available to meet with them); and (3) I do not respond to e-mails. My entire day would be wasted answering e-mails if I bothered answering e-mails throughout the workday.

- If our clients don't have a clear understanding of our communication policies, we will face an endless stream of phone calls and e-mails from them. It's just better that our clients understand our rules for communication from day one, so they are not disappointed when I don't take their unscheduled phone calls.

Your Eight Basic Rights (How to Make Sure Your Injury Lawyer Is Doing His Job)

The "Eight Basic Rights" document explains the rights of the client in a way that no other lawyer will do. Yes, this includes the right to fire your lawyer and the right to get a complete copy of the case file. No other lawyers educate clients about their rights as we do.

Rules for Protecting Your Privacy and Confidentiality Rights

The "Rules for Protecting your Privacy Rights" explains our office procedures for handling medical records and preserving our clients' rights to confidentiality and privacy. This is a compilation of the ten most frequently asked questions by clients about their privacy and confidentiality, such as the rules governing disclosure of case information to family members (we don't do this without our clients' permission).

Why it's done this way: The goal is to be different from every other lawyer. How many lawyers do you know who educate clients about their rights and explain the inner-office procedures? I don't know any. The shock-and-awe package instantly sets us apart from every other law firm and answers our clients' questions, which in turn results in fewer questions and interruptions from our clients.

Client Communication Policy

When new clients contact our office, and I agree to move their cases to "under consideration" in Trialworks, you should mail the seven-page document titled, "The Three Rules of Communication" to the client. In your cover letter, ask the client to sign the last page of the "The Three Rules of Communication," initial the bottom right corner of the first six pages and return the original document in an enclosed, self-addressed, stamped envelope.

When you get the signed "The Three Rules of Communication" back from the new client, you should scan the original under the Memorandum tab in Trialworks and keep the original in a red well with the client's name on it.

I am a total jerk with my time. I do not take inbound, unplanned phone calls.

I do not accept unscheduled or unplanned in-bound phone calls from clients (or just about anyone for that matter). If clients want to speak with me, you should schedule an appointment for the clients to call me between 4:00 p.m. and 5:30 p.m. and allot at least 15 minutes for the phone appointment. You should ask the clients how much time they think they will need for the phone call, and if our clients want more than 15 minutes, you can allot 30 minutes for the phone appointment.

You should ask the clients to send an e-mail or fax to me that specifies the purpose of the phone call. If the clients are elderly or do not have a fax machine or Internet connection, you should ask that they specify the reason for the phone call to you, and you should send me an e-mail with this information.

Why it's done this way: If I accept unscheduled phone calls, I would waste my entire day speaking on the phone without getting any work done. Phone calls are usually a very unproductive use of my time. That's why I do not accept unscheduled phone calls.

John's VIP List

There is a very select group of persons from whom I will accept an unscheduled phone call. I call this my VIP list. With the exception of those on my VIP list, I do not take unscheduled phone calls and you should not ask me if I want to take unplanned calls from anyone not on this list.

My VIP list includes:

- lawyers referring a new case

- claims adjusters with whom I am discussing a settlement

- judges

- my family members—and sometimes I don't take their calls

My Policy about Home Visits with Clients

When disabled clients request a meeting with me, I always meet with them at their home. You should not schedule an office meeting with a disabled client, unless the client specifically requests it.

Why it's done this way: I want to get to know our clients away from the office so I can get a sense of what their life is really like and how their disability affects their everyday life. The only way to do this is through home visits. Our clients appreciate the personal touch of a home visit and it conveys the impression that we care enough to meet them in their home environment.

Interaction with Clients

You should call our clients at least once every four weeks in order to build a more personal relationship with them. Our clients should have a feeling of being "special," a feeling that we care about them and their case. The best way to do this is to communicate with our clients on a regular basis.

If our clients have questions about their case, you should not refer the phone call to me. You should do your best to answer the questions. Your job is to hold our clients' hands and take as much work off my plate as possible. If you're not sure about the status of a case, you should ask the client to schedule a time to speak with you later that day.

E-mails are not the same as a personal phone call. Your communication with our clients should be done primarily by phone or face to face. E-mails are fine as long as you are not communicating with our clients solely through e-mail.

Our Client's Privacy Rights

It is not uncommon that family members of our clients will call you asking for information about the case. Unless our clients give their permission, you cannot even tell their family members that we represent them.

If there is any doubt at all as to who and why someone is asking questions about any aspect of a case (pending or closed cases), no information should be given, even to acknowledge that there is a case. This would be a breach of our clients' rights and our duty to keep such information confidential. When in doubt, you should always ask the attorney handling the file to speak with the person before any information is given.

Why it's done this way: If you convey any information about the case to our clients' families or friends, you are violating our clients' privacy rights.

What You Should Do with a Problem Client

A "problem client" is a client who does not follow our rules.

If you are having difficulty with a client, you should send me an e-mail about the client. I may want to be relieved as counsel by the court. We can't waste our time with clients who do not respect our time and the value we provide them.

Unplanned Phone Calls

On average, I receive between 10 and 15 phone calls a day and each call lasts on average 15 minutes. If I accepted every phone call, I would spend more than half of my day just answering the phone.

So I solve this problem simply by refusing to allow the interruption of unscheduled phone calls.

I will be completely accessible to callers, but on my terms and when I am available. Anyone wanting to speak with me should specify the purpose of the call (ideally set forth in writing) and schedule a time to speak with me when I am available between 4 p.m. and 5:30 p.m.

You should explain that I will always make myself available to our clients, but only on my schedule and when I am available to speak with them without interruption.

Send me a fax or an e-mail explaining the purpose of the phone call. Through this system, I can be prepared to address the questions or concerns the caller has.

Keeping in Touch with Clients

You should be the primary resource for our client. This means that you call our clients at least once a month to ask how they are doing and give them a status report on their case. At least once a month, you should call our clients to ask if they have had any recent medical treatment so you can send the request for updated medical records.

There may be long stretches of time when I am not available to speak with clients due to trials or depositions, so my secretary should be in contact with them on a regular basis.

Our clients may think nothing is happening with their case if they don't hear from us. Of course, we know there is a lot of work taking place behind the scenes, but our clients don't know that.

It's even a good idea to mail our clients copies of their bill of particulars and discovery responses, so they can see for themselves the work that is going on. They will appreciate the updates, and goodwill with our clients is always a good thing.

I want you to develop an emotional bond with our clients. By the end of the case, I want our clients to be raving about you—not me. That's the type of feedback I'm looking for.

3

NEW CASE CALLS

WHEN NEW CLIENTS CALL our law firm, we have one guiding principle: *while the clients are not always right, it is your job to make them feel that way whether or not they are right.*

Do not disagree or argue with clients. Keep in mind that they have never been through a lawsuit before and have little understanding, if any, of how a lawsuit works.

It is your job to show caring in everything that you do. From the way that you answer phones to the way that you greet clients when they come to the office, your caring attitude should shine through. The goal is to give our clients a "Wow!" experience that they've never had from a lawyer.

What Should Happen When a New Client Calls?

When a new client calls the office, the receptionist should first ask, "How were you referred to us?" The new client's answer will determine what happens next.

- If the new client answers, "I was referred by an attorney," the receptionist should transfer the call immediately to my paralegal. The initial screening of the new case is done by my paralegal. New clients referred by a referral partner—namely, a lawyer—should always be given *extra special attention*.

- If the new client was referred by some other source, such as an advertisement and was *not* referred by a lawyer, the phone call should be transferred to Legal Intake Professionals in Nashville, Tennessee.

Why it's done this way: 99 percent of our income is derived from lawyer referrals, so clients referred to us by my referral partners get extra special attention.

What You Should Say during the Initial Phone Call with New Clients

In every case, the first question asked by my paralegal should *always* be, "May I ask how you were referred to us?" The new client may mention my websites (i.e., www.protectingpatientrights.com), social media (e.g., LinkedIn, Facebook, Google Plus, Twitter), my blog (at WordPress), word of mouth from former or present clients, a referral from a lawyer, my newsletters (i.e., *Your Malpractice Insider* and *Lawyer Alert*).

Regardless of how the new client was referred to me, you should document in the Intake Case Manager in Trialworks how the case was referred to me and identify the specific person—for example, "Sally Jones"—who referred the new client to us.

Why it's done this way: If I don't know how new clients are referred to me, it will be impossible to determine what marketing is working for me. If, for example, I receive a new seven-figure case from LinkedIn, I know that my social media is getting results and I will put more of my time and money into social media. It is *crucial* to determine from the beginning of the initial phone conversation with the new clients how they were referred to me.

It is your job to act as a filter to screen new calls that have no merit. Often, calls are made by new "clients" who are only trolling for free information—they have no real injury—or they just want to learn more about malpractice lawsuits. I do not want to take these calls. They are a waste of my time. You should not transfer the no-merit calls to me.

Eight Steps to Answering a Phone Call from a New Client (the Script)

When answering the phone, you must follow a script. You must answer the call exactly as my script is written—yes, that means *word for word*.

My script is not meant to be a suggestion for you, or show you how you *might* want to answer the phone if the mood strikes you. If you were an actress in a movie, you would read your script exactly as it is written, and yes, the same applies to answering the phone.

Answering the phone with a smile on your face is an absolute must. You must be warm and welcoming to our clients and the best way to do that is—you got it—*smile*. If you find this hard to do, you should place a mirror in front of you and focus your attention on the mirror when you are on the phone. This is the best way to remind yourself to smile.

You want to convey a caring and compassionate tone of voice when speaking with new clients.

STEP #1

"Thank you for calling. This is [name of receptionist]. I can help you."

Why it's done this way: By saying, "I can help you," you are starting the initial phone call with a client with a helpful tone that is unique and different from 99 percent of law firm receptionists who answer, "Law Firm. Please hold." Remember, our goal is to be different from everyone else.

STEP #2

"May I ask your name? [First name of client.] Let me be the first to welcome you. Who can we thank for referring you?"

Why it's done this way: The first thing you want to learn from the new client is the name of the referral source, whether that is a lawyer (most common), or a former or current client. It is crucial to get the name of the referral source so referral fees can be paid to referring lawyers in many cases. Since I have a referral-based law practice, the source of the referral of the new client is critical information that you must get early in the phone conversation.

By asking how the new client was referred to us, you accomplish two things: (a) you are instilling in the mind of the new client that we have a referral based law practice—in other words, hopefully, the client will refer new cases to us—and (b) we can document the referral with a letter and send a personalized thank-you letter to the referring lawyer.

Saying "Thank you" to referral sources should be a daily part of our routine. You should remind me to handwrite a thank-you letter to the referring lawyer on the same day that we receive a call from the new client.

Generally, you should always try to call the client by his first name as frequently as possible during the phone conversation—we all love the sound of our name and this conveys a personal touch to the phone call. Your goal is to begin a very personal relationship with the client.

STEP #3

"That's interesting. Most of our clients are referred to us by lawyers."

Why it's done this way: Once again, you are reinforcing in the mind of the new client that we have a referral-based practice and that we welcome referrals from our clients.

STEP #4

"What prompted you to call us?

After the client tells you the reason for the call, you should then say to the client:

"I have some questions to ask you so that we can determine what the next step is for you. Would that be alright?"

In medical malpractice cases, you should obtain the date of the incident—namely, the date of a botched operation or the date when the client believes his medical condition was misdiagnosed, the name of the doctor who treated the client, the nature of the injuries, and the theory of negligence against the doctor. You should enter this information in the Intake Case Manager in Trialworks.

Why it's done this way: The first issue in a new case is whether the statute of limitations has expired. If the statute of limitations has expired, there is no need to get additional information about the case.

By getting the names of the treating physicians and hospitals, you will know where to send release authorizations to get the client's medical records. In complicated cases with multiple treating physicians, you should ask the client to send an e-mail or letter with the names and addresses of treating physicians and hospitals, the approximate dates of treatment with each doctor and hospital, and a statement of the client's complaint against the doctor or hospital. (This communication is protected by the attorney-client privilege.) This will help us make sure we get all of the relevant medical records.

You should ask the following questions:

- "Have you discussed this case with any other lawyers?"

- "When did this happen?"

- "Where did this occur?"

- "Tell me exactly what happened."

- "What were the injuries from the malpractice?"

- "Do you have any of the medical records concerning your treatment?"

Additionally, you need to get the client's full name, address, e-mail address, date of birth, Social Security number, home, cell and work phone numbers, and the name of the injured party (if different from the caller). The client's biographical information should be entered for every new case call in the New Intake Manager in Trialworks.

Practice tip: Always get the caller's e-mail address. With the e-mail address, we have a way to communicate immediately with the client after the phone call—namely, "Thank you again for calling us. We will mail John's book, *The Seven Deadly Mistakes of Malpractice Victims*, to you today. Just in case you want the book right away, we are attaching an electronic copy of John's book with this e-mail. As always, please do not hesitate to call us if you have any questions." New clients will appreciate the immediate feedback by getting an e-mail after the initial phone call.

Very Important!

If the new client sustained a catastrophic injury or the new case involves death, find me and get me on the phone! Nothing is more important. If I am on the phone with a judge, interrupt me! In *big* cases, you should schedule a home visit *that day* so I can meet with the client. If you tell clients that we will get back to them soon, they will call the next lawyer with the biggest advertisement in the yellow pages.

STEP #5

You should always explain the next step in the process. For example, you might say, "We will e-mail an HIPAA power-of-attorney form to you that you should sign before a notary public and return to us by mail. Once we have the HIPAA power of attorney from you, we will request your medical records from the physicians and hospitals. It usually takes two to four weeks to get the medical records."

Why it's done this way: By explaining the process, the clients will know what to expect and how long it will take before we contact them again. You do not want to end the conversation without making sure the clients know exactly what will happen next. You should send an e-mail to them immediately after the phone call to reinforce the next step in the process.

STEP #6

"By the way, have you read John's book? John is the author of the book *The Seven Deadly Mistakes of Malpractice Victims.* May I send you John's book?"

Why it's done this way: The book offer hammers home the concept that the new client found the right lawyer—namely, the guy who "wrote the book."

STEP #7

"We look forward to working for you. If for some reason you decide that you do not want us to work for you, will you let us know?"

Why it's done this way: You want clients to make a *verbal contract* that they will not hang up the phone and call another lawyer. I don't want to spend time and money on a new case if the clients are "lawyer shopping." Getting the clients to say yes to the verbal contract gives at least some commitment by the clients that they are not going to call the next lawyer they see in a TV lawyer commercial.

STEP #8

"Did I answer all of your questions? Is there anything else I can help you with? Thank you again for calling."

Why it's done this way: I call this the "Wow!" closing. By this point, you want new clients to believe that there is no question they have found the best lawyer for their case.

What Makes a Good Case?

A common element in a good case is a *big injury*. A big injury is one that is disabling and will have a long-lasting impact on our client's life. If the client has a significant injury that has only a temporary impact, I will not take that case 99 percent of the time.

When you take a phone call from a new client, the thought in the back of your mind should always be, "Does this person have a big injury?" If not, it's very unlikely that I will be interested in his case.

What Should Happen When a New Client Comes to Our Office without an Appointment?

I do not take unscheduled, walk-in appointments—for anyone. If new clients arrive at our office without an appointment, you should get their information: name, address, phone number, and so on, and the basic information about their case. If the new clients have a case that might have merit (fat chance in most cases), you should tell the clients that they should call our office to make an appointment to speak with me (just like everyone else).

Why it's done this way: Unscheduled walk-in appointments are never acceptable. These clients are high maintenance and virtually never have a case that I will accept. Unscheduled, walk-in appointments are an interruption to my workday and I do not accept them.

How to Enter Data from New Case Calls

Before you transfer a phone call from a new client to me, you should make sure you enter the client's background information—name, address, phone number, and so on—in the Intake Case Manager of Trialworks, also known as the "Intake Wizard."

Why it's done this way: I do not want to enter the client's background information every time a new client calls. This is a waste of my time. You should always enter this information in the Trialworks Intake Case Manager before you transfer the phone call to me.

Every incoming call from a new client (whether the new client has a personal injury, DWI, or divorce case) should be entered into Trialworks through the Intake Case Manager (see upper right corner of the Trialworks screen for the "Intake Wizard" icon). Even if you know that we will not accept the case, you should enter the client's information in the Intake Case Manager in Trialworks.

A "client" is anyone calling my office asking for advice, even if that person is only trolling for free information or may be mentally unstable.

When you take a phone call from a new client, you should always enter the client's name, address, e-mail address, date of birth, Social Security number, name of the injured person, the date of the incident, the type of case (medical malpractice, motor vehicle accident, premises liability, etc.) the date the statute of limitations will expire (if you know), and a brief summary of the relevant events. You should enter this information in the Trialworks Intake Case Manager.

Under the Comments tab of the Intake Case Manager, you should enter your name (so I can tell who entered the information), the date when you spoke with the new client, and your initial plan of action for the case—for example, "verbally rejected the case and will follow up with a rejection letter" or "will get medical records and open a new case in Trialworks."

In Section Two of the Intake Case Manager, you should always ask new clients how they were referred to the firm, such as Internet, lawyer referral, client referral, yellow pages and so on. Once you have this information, you should document the source of the new business in the Trialworks Intake Case Manager.

Why it's done this way: We must keep careful track of every new client who calls us, even if they want to sue McDonald's for having soggy french fries. This will allow us to keep track of the number of new case calls, the source of new clients, and what type of marketing is generating the best new cases.

After you take the background information from the new client, you should transfer the phone call to me. I will complete the rest of the information about the new client's case in the Trialworks Intake Case Manager.

However, it is often the case that I will not be available to speak with the new client. If I am not available to speak with the client, you should take a statement describing the nature of the claim—namely, what happened and the injuries sustained by our new client.

What You Should Do after the Initial Intake from a New Client

After you enter the data about the new client in the Intake Case Manager in Trialworks, you should do one of two things:

If I reject the case, you should mail a rejection letter to the client and send a copy of the rejection letter to the referring lawyer. A copy of the scanned original of the rejection letter should be electronically filed in the shared F file in the network.

If I want to review the case for merit, you should send an e-mail to our receptionist asking her to open the new file in Trialworks as "under consideration." After a new file is created for the case in Trialworks, you should not enter any new information in that file in the Intake Case Manager.

I will make a decision on whether to reject a new case or transfer the new case to "under consideration" in Trialworks on the first day the new client calls us. I will give you clear directions on whether I want to reject the case or open the case in Trialworks on the same day that we receive the phone call.

When a new case is entered in Trialworks as "under consideration," you should mail my introduction letter to our new client together with my audio CD, "What You Can Expect to Happen Next in Your Injury Case." This CD describes the procedures of a personal injury lawsuit from beginning to end.

Why it's done this way: The introduction letter and the audio CD answer most of the questions posed by new clients, so you and I will not need to spend time answering the same questions. Additionally, new clients get a little surprise present in the mail that no other lawyers send. This creates an impression with our new clients that they hired a unique lawyer (which hopefully they have).

Opening a New Case in Trialworks

When you create a new case in Trialworks, you should always open the case in the name of the client who will bring the lawsuit. You should not create the new case in the name of the decedent in a wrongful death case.

Tracking New Case Calls

On the first Friday of every month, you should send me an e-mail listing the number of new case calls for that month and the source of the new clients, such as website, social media, lawyer referral, client referral, newspaper advertisement, and so on. Your e-mail to me should indicate how many prospective cases were opened in Trialworks—as "under consideration"—and how many were rejected.

Why it's done this way: I need to keep track of how I am getting new business and without this information, I won't be able to tell what marketing is working. My marketing dollars are budgeted, so I need to know what marketing sources are getting new clients to call me.

What You Should Ask New Clients to Do When Their Cases Are Moved to "Under Consideration" in Trialworks

On the first day a new client calls us, I will make a decision. Either (a) the new case is rejected and a rejection letter is mailed to the client, or (b) the new case will be opened in Trialworks as "under consideration." There is no third option.

If I tell you to move a new case into Trialworks as "under consideration" (option b), you call or e-mail the client to ask that he/she do two things: (1) write a narrative summary that explains in detail the nature of the new case—namely, the basis of the complaint—and (2) ask the client to write a list of all medical providers, including hospitals and physicians, who treated him/her, with dates of treatment.

The narrative summary form, or intake form, asks nine questions:

- When did the medical mistake occur?

- Name the physician, hospital or medical provider responsible for the medical mistake.

- Describe the medical mistake in as much detail as possible.

- List the names and addresses of the doctors and hospitals that treated you for your injuries.

- Have you recovered from your injury?

- Do you have any permanent injury caused by the medical mistake? If so, please describe the continuing injury that you have.

- When was the last time that you received medical treatment for your injury?

- Do you have any of the medical records? If so, please provide us with a copy of the medical records.

- Are you still being treated by the doctor who made the medical mistake? If not, when was the last date on which you received medical treatment from the doctor?

You should explain to our new clients that the information contained in the narrative summary, or intake form, is protected by the attorney-client privilege and will not be disclosed to anyone outside our law firm. You should also explain to our new clients that they should shred any copies that they make of the narrative summary in order to ensure that it is not disclosed to others.

Why it's done this way: The narrative summary will help me get a better grasp of the new case and the issues that the client wants me to focus on. The list of medical providers will help us get all of the medical records. No need to worry; both documents are protected from disclosure as attorney-client communications. This just makes our job easier.

Procedures for New Motor Vehicle Accident Cases

I expect you to handle all of the initial steps in new motor vehicle accident cases. I should not be involved at all in the initial setup of a new case involving a motor vehicle accident. It is your job to prepare and mail the paperwork in the initial setup of the new case.

There are six steps that you should take in every new motor vehicle accident case (without asking me what to do):

- Mail the application for no-fault insurance benefits to the no-fault insurer;

- Send a letter to our client's underinsurance (SUM) carrier informing them of our client's potential underinsurance claim;

- Obtain a copy of the police accident report and get photographs of the vehicles and the accident scene/location. You should ask for my permission before you hire a private investigator;

- Mail a "letter of representation" to the tortfeasor's insurance carrier to inform that company that we represent the client and ask for the disclosure of the tortfeasor's insurance coverage for bodily injury;

- If a traffic ticket was issued to the tortfeasor, you should send a letter to the justice court where the ticket is pending in order to notify the court that our client sustained a significant physical injury in the accident. You should find out the date and time of the court appearance relative to the traffic ticket and you should make sure that someone from our office attends the court appearance.

Why it's done this way: If you do not notify the court of our client's physical injuries, it is very likely the court will accept a plea reduction of the traffic ticket for a trivial offense—for example, parking on pavement or failure to wear a seat belt. If the court is aware that our client sustained a physical injury in the accident, the court will not accept a plea reduction and the tortfeasor will be forced to plead guilty to the driving infraction. The tortfeasor's guilty plea to a violation of the Vehicle and Traffic Law is very helpful in proving liability in our client's lawsuit.

You can get the names of the tortfeasor's insurance company from the insurance code on the police accident report. You should also check the bottom of the police accident report for the names of eyewitnesses to the accident. If there were eyewitnesses, you should send me an e-mail to ask whether I want to assign a private investigator to get a sworn statement from the eyewitness.

You should ask our client to e-mail or fax the declaration page from his automobile insurer, so you can verify our client's coverage for bodily injury and underinsurance. You should always send a notice of underinsurance coverage to the underinsurance auto insurer, even if you have no idea whether underinsurance applies.

You should have new clients sign a power of attorney allowing us to sign release authorizations for their medical records, and request a list of our clients' medical providers. You should then send written requests for all of our clients' medical records that relate to the treatment only from the date of the accident to the present.

When a new motor vehicle accident case is accepted, you should take the following six steps without asking me to do anything. I expect you to take these six steps without any help from me. I should not be involved in the initial set up of new motor vehicle accident cases.

Why it's done this way: Particularly in new cases, you should mail copies of our correspondence to our clients. The correspondence keeps our clients informed of the work we are doing for them and reduces the phone calls we get from clients asking what is going on with their cases.

Retainer Agreement

You should not send a retainer agreement to a new client until I have accepted the case. Once I inform you that I have accepted the case, you should prepare the retainer agreement in triplicate and the memorandum regarding the division of fees. The retainer agreements should be mailed to the client for signing; the client should be instructed to keep one original and return two originals to you.

You should then mail one original retainer agreement and two memoranda regarding the division of fees to the referring lawyer for signing. You should instruct the referring lawyer to sign the original memorandum, keep one original for his records, and return one original to you.

You should always identify the referring lawyer by his name— for example, "John Smith, Esq."—rather than the name of his law firm unless the referring lawyer asks that you list his law firm as the referring lawyer.

Rejection Letters

Every case that is rejected should be recorded in a rejection letter. The form letter for rejections should be used for every rejection. You should not change the content of the rejection letter.

You should scan and sign copies of rejection letters and keep them in a digital format instead of paper copies. The fact that the letter is signed serves as an indication to us that it was sent to the client.

You should scan all documents provided by prospective clients into Trialworks under the appropriate tab, scan the signed copy of the rejection letter into Trialworks, return to the prospective clients any personal papers they provided and shred the remainder of the file.

If the case was referred by a lawyer, you should always "cc" the referring lawyer and mail a copy of the rejection letter to the referring lawyer. You should always keep the referring lawyer informed of our decision whether to accept or reject the case.

Sometimes I may create a case-specific rejection letter for cases referred by a referring lawyer. It is only in this rare situation that the content of the rejection letter will be changed.

Why it's done this way: If there is no rejection letter, we have no proof that we did not reject the case. This leaves our law firm open to legal malpractice claims that we missed a statute of limitations by failing to file the lawsuit.

Referring Lawyers

When new cases are referred by lawyers, you should ask the referring lawyers whether they want to be listed as co-counsel on all documents served and filed in the lawsuit—pleadings, discovery responses, motions, and so on. If the referring lawyers want to be listed as co-counsel on the litigation documents, you must send copies of all litigation documents to the referring lawyers.

By listing the referring lawyers as co-counsel on the summons and complaint, you will ensure that the referring lawyers receive copies of all documents served by the defendants during the lawsuit. It is the rare situation that a referring lawyer wants to be listed as co-counsel, but you should let him/her know that this is an option *before* we file the summons and complaint.

Why it's done this way: Our goal is to keep the referring lawyer informed about the status of the case. Hence, I have no problem with the designation of the referring lawyer as co-counsel on all documents that are served in the lawsuit.

Acknowledgment of Referral of a New Client from Lawyers

When I receive a referral of a new case from a lawyer, you must confirm the referral with a letter mailed to the referring lawyer within 24–48 hours of the new referral. The form letter acknowledges the referral and thanks the referring lawyer for the new case and promises to keep him informed of our decision on whether to accept or reject the case.

Why it's done this way: Referring lawyers are the life-blood of my business and it is crucial to keep them informed of the status of our work. *The ultimate measure of success is a committed referral partner*, so you want to keep our referral partners informed of the status of the case as often as possible.

Tracking Referrals to Other Counsel

When I refer a new client to another law firm, you should always record the referral relationship in a letter to the outside counsel. The letter should read, "I am referring Mr. Jones to you on a referral basis" and specify the division of the legal fee. My customary referral fee is one-third of the total legal fees.

I have a database in Trialworks, used only for the purpose of tracking cases that I refer to other counsel. After a new case is referred to other counsel, you should send a letter to the outside counsel, once every 21 days, asking if a decision has been made whether to accept the referral.

If the outside counsel accepts the referral of the new client, you should always ask the outside counsel to list me as co-counsel on all documents that are filed in the lawsuit, and most importantly, on the summons and complaint.

Why it's done this way: When I am listed as co-counsel on all of the litigation documents, the defense counsel and the court will be required to send copies of all of their correspondence, and motion and discovery responses to me. By doing this, I will be kept informed of the status of the case, even if I never get any updates from the outside counsel to whom I referred the case.

You should also insist that I be listed as the referring lawyer in the retainer agreement and that the division of the legal fee is specified in a separate agreement between the outside lawyer and me.

Why it's done this way: If the referral relationship is not set forth in a written agreement, I am not entitled to a referral fee, which means we don't get paid and go out of business in short order. The outside attorney will screw me out of a referral fee unless I protect my rights by documenting the referral of the case, and the amount of the referral fee, in a written agreement that is signed by the outside attorney.

After the outside lawyer has accepted the referral, you should mail a letter requesting an update about the status of the case once every four months.

If the outside lawyer isn't doing his job, neither am I. The legal malpractice of the outside lawyer is the same as legal malpractice by yours truly—in other words, if the outside lawyer is missing deadlines during discovery, I am "on the hook" for his legal malpractice. That's why you should check with the outside lawyer for a status of the case once every four months.

Referrals to Out-of-State Lawyers

When new clients need an attorney outside New York, you should *never* tell them that "John doesn't practice in your state." Instead, you should explain to the client that I accept new cases across the country and that I co-counsel with lawyers in cases that are brought outside New York State.

You should then send me an e-mail asking for the name of a lawyer to whom I can refer the new client.

Why it's done this way: The referral of a personal injury case to an attorney practicing outside New York State is just as good, if not better, than having a New York State client. Why, you ask? I can refer the case to another lawyer and collect a referral fee at the end of the case while doing virtually no work and spending no money on the case. There's nothing better than that.

4

DISCOVERY, MOTIONS, AND LIENS

Discovery

COMMENCEMENT OF THE LAWSUIT

After the summons and complaint have been served, you should enter in the calendar the defendant's deadlines to serve answers. If we do not receive an answer from the defendants by their deadline, you should send me an e-mail informing me that the deadline for an answer expired.

It is your job to make sure all of the defendants have been served with the summons and complaint within 120 days of the filing of the summons and complaint.

You should always make sure we possess an acknowledgment of service from each of the defendants. If you do not possess an acknowledgment accepting service by mail from each of the defendants within 60 days after the filing of the lawsuit, you should send me an e-mail stating, "We have not received an acknowledgment of service from defendant

Mr. Jones. I will have Mr. Jones personally served with the summons and complaint."

Instead of asking me what to do, you have my permission to hire a process server to personally serve the summons and complaint upon the defendant if you do not receive an acknowledgment of service within 60 days of the filing of the lawsuit.

Why it's done this way: The lawsuit will be automatically dismissed if we do not complete service of the summons and complaint within 120 days of the filing of the summons and complaint.

CAPTION OF PLEADINGS

The names of the parties should be typed in lower case with the exception of the initial letters.

DEADLINES

Deadlines are extremely important, particularly deadlines contained in a preliminary conference discovery order. I can be sued for legal malpractice for failing to serve discovery responses and a bill of particulars by the deadline in a preliminary conference scheduling order. You should be aware of deadlines and make sure you meet them.

If there are any deadlines approaching, such as a deadline to serve opposition papers to a motion or the deadline to file a motion for summary judgment or the note of issue, you should enter the deadline in the calendar and send me weekly reminders of the deadline by e-mail.

Within one week of the deadline, you should send me an e-mail with subject line, "TOP PRIORITY—DISCOVERY RESPONSES DUE."

EXTENSIONS OF COURT-ORDERED DEADLINES FOR DISCOVERY

If you cannot complete discovery within the court-ordered deadline contained in the preliminary conference stipulation and order, you should call the defendant's counsel to select new dates for the completion of discovery. Once you have a new date that is agreeable to the defense counsel, you should prepare a letter to the court requesting the extension of the discovery deadline.

I hate extensions and adjournments! But realistically, there will be occasions when we need to extend the discovery deadlines, and when that happens, you must make sure you request the extension of the deadline *before* the deadline expires.

Why it's done this way: If we do not respect discovery deadlines in a preliminary conference stipulation and order, we cannot expect the defendant's counsel to comply with the deadlines either. Many judges, particularly in a federal court, will not grant extensions of discovery deadlines *unless* you request the extension before the deadline expires.

ADJOURNMENTS

You should never adjourn anything without my permission. My goal is to keep cases on the track to trial and *adjournments are the mortal enemy of this goal.*

The defense lawyers will try their best to adjourn everything they can. Your job is to just say no. You should not adjourn anything.

HOW TO DEAL WITH DIFFICULT DEFENSE COUNSEL

It is inevitable that defense counsel will not cooperate with you in scheduling depositions and serving discovery responses. The job of the defense is to delay and adjourn everything, and they are experts at doing this. So, what can you do about it?

When you serve the plaintiff's discovery responses and demands with the notice of commencement of medical malpractice (in mal-

practice cases only), the court will schedule a preliminary conference for the purpose of scheduling deadlines for the completion
of discovery. Almost all defense lawyers ignore the deadlines in the
court's scheduling order, but you should treat the scheduling order as
the Ten Commandments for the case.

When you receive a scheduling order, you should enter all of the
deadlines in the calendar. If you cannot serve a discovery response by
the deadline in the scheduling order, you must send a written request
to the court for an extension of the deadline in the order *before* the
deadline expires.

Why it's done this way: If we do not take scheduling orders
seriously, we look unprofessional and we cannot expect the court to
enforce a deadline if we don't meet our court-imposed deadlines. It is
your job to make sure that we meet all of the deadlines in the court's
scheduling orders.

BILLS OF PARTICULARS AND DISCOVERY RESPONSES

Big Picture Goals for Their Cases: A victory for our clients is getting
their cases to trial within 18 months of the date when we accepted the
case—namely, the date when client signed the retainer agreement.
Our clients will not get the result they deserve until the trial. Getting
the case to trial is our single most important goal in every case.

Why it's done this way: *Until our clients' cases get to trial, there
will be no money.* Our clients won't get paid and neither will we. The
goal is to move cases as aggressively as possible toward trial while
sparing no delay tactics. You will face an endless number of lame
excuses from defense counsel to adjourn depositions and trials, and
it's your job to insist upon strict compliance with the court's preliminary scheduling order for discovery.

PRELIMINARY COURT CONFERENCE REGARDING DISCOVERY

After the court has notified you of a date for the preliminary scheduling conference, you should fax, e-mail, or mail a letter to the defense counsel asking for at least three alternative dates when that defense counsel will be available for the depositions of the plaintiff and defendant as well as for any nonparty depositions.

In your letter you should inform the defense counsel that you will ask the judge to "so-order" specific dates for the depositions of the parties and nonparties, and if the defense counsel does not provide alternative dates to you, you will assume that counsel will be generally available on a date that you select.

Why it's done this way: The biggest obstacle posed by the defense counsel is scheduling the depositions. More often than not, the defense counsel will have their secretary tell you that they refuse to schedule the defendant's depositions until after the plaintiff's depositions have been completed. This is *utter nonsense*. For this reason, you should always get alternative dates for depositions from the defense counsel before the preliminary scheduling conference with the court.

Three days before the preliminary scheduling conference, you should send a letter via facsimile to the defense lawyers asking that they notify you via fax if they claim that there are any outstanding issues in discovery, such as documents or discovery responses that have not been provided by the plaintiff. The letter to the defense counsel states that I will assume that there are no outstanding discovery issues if that defense counsel does not respond to my letter.

Why it's done this way: I need to know whether there are any outstanding discovery issues *before* the preliminary scheduling conference. By sending this letter, I will be alerted to discovery issues that will be addressed at the preliminary conference schedule before the conference. Hence, I will be prepared to discuss the discovery issue at the preliminary conference or I can hand deliver the requested discovery responses or documents to the defense counsel on the day of the preliminary conference. The goal is to address any objections or issues raised by the defense counsel before the preliminary conference so I can get an expedited and streamlined discovery schedule from the court.

BILLS OF PARTICULARS

I will prepare the allegations of negligence and the list of injuries in the plaintiff's bill of particulars. You do not need to do that (this is your choice).

You are responsible for preparing the remaining parts of the plaintiff's bill of particulars. You must specifically list all of the plaintiff's medical providers with the dates of treatment.

Why it's done this way: I do not want to spend time making sure the list of medical providers and dates of treatment in a bill of particulars are correct. This is your job. I will only focus upon the allegations of negligence and the list of the plaintiff's injuries in a bill of particulars, and I will assume you have done a bang-up job with the rest of the bill of particulars.

If you have questions about how you should answer the demand for a bill of particulars, you should call the client. For example, how long were you confined to your home after the injury, or how long were you confined to bed? You shouldn't ask me to answer these questions. It is your job to call the client, go through the questions in the bill of particulars, and provide very specific answers.

Don't forget, I want our clients to rave about you (not me). The only way to develop a close bond with our clients is to communicate with them. You get the picture.

The list of injuries in the bill of particulars must provide a complete list of our client's injuries and also list the future consequences of the injuries. For example, if our client sustained a fracture of his knee, you should include among the injuries: "Increased likelihood of future arthritis in the knee." If you do not list the future consequences of the injuries, such as "increased likelihood of cosmetic surgery to improve the appearance of the facial scars," we cannot submit evidence of the future consequences of the injuries at the trial.

DISCOVERY RESPONSES

You should prepare all of the discovery responses and discovery demands, including a cross-notice of video deposition and a notice of the plaintiff's availability for a physical examination.

Deadlines for the service of discovery responses should be taken seriously. If you are unable to meet a deadline for discovery responses, you should request an extension from the defense lawyer.

You should list all of the questions in the plaintiff's discovery responses and provide each answer directly below the question.

Why it's done this way: The question-and-answer format for discovery responses allows me to determine context for every answer. When I am in trial, I do not want to hunt around for the discovery demand for every discovery response.

There is no provision of the CPLR or the Uniform Rules of Trial Courts relating to the exchange of medical records that requires that I provide copies of medical records to defense counsel in a paper format. If it is a two-page document, you should send the medical records in a paper format. Once the medical records get to be larger than 10 pages, it doesn't make sense to send anything other than a compact disc that contains the medical records in an electronic format.

Why it's done this way: By providing documents—namely, medical records—in a digital format on a compact disc (instead of paper copies), we are saving the time and expense of photocopying large records. Also, printing a large document ties up the use of the large printers.

When I give you the signed discovery responses, you should serve them on defense counsel by mail on the same day that you receive them. It is not acceptable to hold onto the signed discovery responses for two or three days after you receive them.

OBJECTIONS TO THE DEFENDANT'S DISCOVERY DEMANDS

In virtually all cases, the defense lawyer will serve a discovery demand that seeks inappropriate and objectionable documents from our client.

I will do the initial review of new discovery demands, identify the inquiries that are objectionable, and then have you prepare a letter with the appropriate objections. The letter specifying my objections must be served within twenty (20) days of the service of the discovery demand.

When I object to a demand for a bill of particulars or discovery demand, I usually cite cases that specifically hold that the inquiry is improper. For example, with a request for information about lack of informed consent—namely, what information should have been conveyed to the patient—I object and cite cases that hold that such inquiries are improper for a bill of particulars.

Why it's done this way: If you do not mail a letter to defense counsels objecting to their discovery demands within 20 days, our client waives his objections to the demands. Even if the defendant's discovery demands seek improper disclosure such as income tax records, substance abuse, or child protective service records, we waive our objection if we do not serve a timely objection upon defense counsel.

There is no question that, at a minimum, a *timely* written objection to defense counsel is necessary. The objection *must be served* within 20 days of the date of the defendant's discovery demand.

When the defendants serve objectionable demands for bills of particulars, we need to identify those objectionable demands and send a letter of objection immediately. In the case of a bill of particulars, the objection letter must be served within 30 days of the date of the demand and reiterated when we serve our answers to the demand.

As soon as we receive a demand for expert disclosure and/or a demand for a bill of particulars (particularly in a medical malpractice case), please take a quick look at the demands and *immediately* send a letter of objection if one is needed.

OBJECT TO DISCOVERY DEMANDS SEEKING ACCESS TO SOCIAL MEDIA

New York courts have uniformly held that a defendant is not entitled to the blocked content of a plaintiff's Facebook site by the mere existence of the site itself.

The defendants may not obtain discovery of blocked social media postings absent the existence of some articulable basis for believing that the private content is material and relevant to the plaintiff's litigation claims, such as information giving rise to the belief that the blocked content "contradicts or conflicts with the plaintiff's alleged restrictions, disabilities, losses, or other claims" (*Tapp v. NYS Urban Development*, 102 A.D.3d 620 [1st Dep't 2013]). In the absence of such a factual predicate, the courts will deny the Facebook-related discovery.

Even when a factual predicate exists for the discovery of blocked social media, a defendant will still not be permitted access to a plaintiff's private postings unless the discovery demand is limited to information that is truly material and relevant to the contested claims of the action (*Kregg v. Maldonado*, 98 A.D.3d 1289 [4th Dep't 2012]). For defendants, there will often be no basis for seeking the disclosure of private social media postings during the early phase of a lawsuit.

Practice tip: Object in writing immediately when served with the pro forma discovery demand seeking disclosure from the plaintiff's private social media sites. If you do not object within 20 days, you may waive the objection.

DISCOVERY OF ELECTRONIC RECORDS

In more than 50% of hospitals, medical records are maintained in an electronic format, a/k/a "electronic medical records". In those cases, you should request disclosure of the "audit trail" of the electronic records.

The audit trail will show the history of all changes to the medical records. The audit trail will show all of the additions, changes and deletions to the patient's electronic medical records and the date and time that the medical record was changed. For example, the audit trail will show that Dr. Jones added notations to the patient's medical record on December 3rd (five weeks after the patient was discharged from the hospital).

If emails are part of the computer system (as opposed to an external system for emails like gmail), there will be an audit trail for emails. Within the metadata, there will be information showing the date the email was created, the history of changes to the email and when those changes were made.

Do you need a computer forensic examination to get the audit trail? Not always. You can get a paper copy of the audit trail that will display the date of the additions, changes and deletions to the patient's electronic medical records and emails. If, on the other hand, you want to get the metadata, you will need a forensic computer examination.

How do you make sense of the audit trail? You should serve a notice for the deposition of the "IT guy", or the go-to guy who knows everything about the defendant's computer systems. You should ask the IT expert whether emails are external to the electronic medical record system and ask him to describe the audit trail.

Don't forget to serve a preservation letter for the electronically stored information as soon as you accept the case. The preservation letter that I serve begins:

As critical evidence in this case exists in the form of Electronically Stored Information ("ESI") contained in the computer systems of Albany Medical Center Hospital, this is a notice and demand that such evidence must be immediately preserved and retained by Albany Medical Center Hospital until further written notice from the undersigned. This request is essential, as a paper printout of text contained in a computer file does not completely reflect all information contained within the electronic file.

Additionally, the continued operation of the computer systems identified herein will likely result in the destruction of relevant ESI due to the fact that electronic evidence can be easily altered, deleted or otherwise modified. The failure to preserve and retain the ESI outlined in this notice constitutes spoliation of evidence and will subject Albany Medical Center Hospital to legal claims for damages and /or evidentiary and monetary sanctions.

Unless and until all potentially relevant ESI has been preserved, Albany Medical Center Hospital must refrain from operating (or removing or altering fixed or external drives and media attached thereto) standalone personal computers, network stations, notebook and/or laptop computers relating to our client, Mrs. Jones.

STATUTE OF LIMITATIONS

You should keep track of the date when the statute of limitations will expire in all of our cases. Once we are within two months of the date when the statute of limitations will expire, you should send me weekly e-mail reminders with the subject line, "TOP PRIORITY—SOL."

REQUESTS FOR ADDITIONAL MEDICAL RECORDS BY DEFENSE COUNSEL

Whenever the defendant's counsel requests release authorizations for medical records for treatment that occurred before the defendant's negligence, you should make sure that we request the same medical records.

Why it's done this way: We do not want the defendant's attorneys to have medical records that we don't have.

DEFENSE MEDICAL EXAMINATIONS

Our clients should *never* attend a defense medical examination alone. You should make sure that someone from our office such as a secretary, paralegal, or errand boy attends the defense medical examination with our client.

Why it's done this way: If our client attends a defense medical examination alone, the defense doctor will ask inappropriate questions about the accident such as "Describe the accident," or "Tell me about your bipolar disorder." Such questions are highly improper for a defense exam. However, with no one present to protect our client from such improper questions, the defense doctor will take advantage. You can bet that the defense doctor is taking audio and video of the defense examination from the moment our client parks his car and everything that our client does and says will be recorded by surveillance video.

NOTE OF ISSUE

You must make sure the note of issue is filed before the deadline specified in the scheduling order. If discovery has not been completed by the deadline in the scheduling order, you should prepare a letter for my signature asking the court for an extension of the deadline for the filing of the note of issue and specifying why more time is needed for discovery.

With very few exceptions, I always file a demand for a *nonjury* trial in the note of issue. Unless I specifically ask for a jury demand, you should always assume that the note of issue should request a nonjury trial.

However, we must always get our client's consent to file a nonjury note of issue.

Why it's done this way: Our clients have a constitutional right to a jury trial and we cannot neglect this important right. Hence, you should get our client's consent to file a nonjury trial with a letter signed by the client.

DISCOVERY DEMANDS FOR AUTHORIZATIONS AFTER THE NOTE OF ISSUE

Defense lawyers often request authorizations for medical records and non-medical records after the filing of the note of issue. When this happens, you must object in writing within 20 days.

The filing of the note of issue cuts off any further discovery. While you must serve any updated medical records on defense counsel after the filing of the note issue, defense lawyers have no right to authorizations for updated medical records once the note of issue has been filed.

There is one exception: defense lawyers are entitled to authorizations that are needed for trial subpoenas. If a defense lawyer requests an authorization for a trial subpoena, it is okay to provide it to them.

Motions

If we receive a motion from the defense counsel, it is your job to keep track of the deadline for me to serve our opposition papers. You should give me e-mail reminders of the deadline twice a week as the deadline approaches, with the subject line, "TOP PRIORITY— MOTION DEADLINE."

When you receive the decision and order, it is your job to file the decision and order with the county clerk's office. Once you get a date-stamped copy of the decision and order from the county clerk, you must serve a copy of the date-stamped decision and order upon defense counsel by mail.

PERSONAL SERVICE BY MAIL

As an alternative to serving a summons and complaint by personally delivering it to a defendant, CPLR Section 312-a permits service by mailing a copy of the summons and complaint to the defendant, by first-class mail, together with two copies of a statement by service by mail and acknowledgment, together with a prepaid envelope, addressed to the sender, for a return of the acknowledgment.

If the defendant signs and returns the acknowledgment, the time frame within which to answer begins to run upon the mailing of the receipt.

If the defendant fails to sign and return the receipt, you should have him served personally, and I will obtain an immediate judgment for the cost of service.

When using this method, you should keep in mind that all entities to be served (i.e., each doctor, or the doctor's corporation) must be separately sent a complete package addressed to them.

Why it's done this way: Our clients will save a ton of money on process service by serving pleadings and subpoenas by mail and the defendants and subpoena recipients almost always accept service by mail. This is a no-brainer.

HOW TO SEND THE MOTION PAPERS TO THE COURT

If I prepare the original notice of motion and affirmation, you must send those documents to the county clerk's office because we have to pay a $45 filing fee on the motion. Remember, you do not pay fees to the Supreme Court clerk.

The cover letter to the county clerk in this situation should state: "Enclosed is a notice of motion and affirmation that are returnable before Judge (whoever) on (whatever date). Also enclosed is our check in the amount of $45.00 in payment of the required filing fee. Please transfer the motion papers to the Supreme Court clerk's office so that they may be forwarded on to the judge."

You must also pay filing fees to the county clerk for cross-motions because another filing fee is required. Filing fees are never paid to the Supreme Court clerk.

MOTION PRACTICE IN MOTOR VEHICLE CASES

In motor vehicle cases, it is often the case that I will need to make a motion for partial summary judgment on the issue of liability. It is your job to keep track of our deadline for making the motion for summary judgment.

Under the CPLR, I have 120 days to serve the summary judgment motion from the date the note of issue is filed. However, the court often imposes a shorter deadline, such as 30 or 60 days, after the filing of the note of issue. You should enter the deadline in our calendar and within 30 days of the deadline, you should send e-mails to me on a weekly basis reminding me of the deadline.

WHAT TO DO AFTER THE MOTION IS DECIDED

After judges have ruled on motions, they normally return all of the original motion papers to the prevailing party. Now, it is time to send all of the original papers to the county clerk to be filed.

Liens

MEDICARE LIENS

As soon as the lawsuit is filed, you must request a lien amount from Medicare and/or Medicaid. There are three steps to getting a final lien amount from Medicare.

STEP #1

To start, you should call the Medicare coordination of benefits contractor (1-800-999-1118) and provide the requested information about our client—namely, name, address, date of birth, Social

Security number, Medicare number, and the nature of the injury. This will result in the claim being added to the Medicare recovery system and being referred to the Medicare secondary payer recovery contractor (MSPRC) from whom the final lien reimbursement will be obtained.

You should then fax or mail a letter to the MSPRC at P.O. Box 138832, Oklahoma City, Oklahoma 73113 (fax #405-869-3309) requesting a conditional payment letter showing the Medicare payments made related to the claim. Along with this letter, you must send a form titled "Proof of Representation" and an authorization signed by the client allowing the disclosure of his Medicare information to us. Within 65 days the "Proof of Representation" form will generate a response from Medicare known as a conditional payment letter. The conditional payment letter will have an itemized list of each expense made by Medicare relating to our client's injuries.

If you do not receive the conditional payment letter from the MSPRC within 65 days, you should call the MSPRC to check on the status (1-800-677-7220). The MSPRC will answer phone calls between 8:00 a.m. and 8:00 p.m., but the best time to call (with the shortest wait time) is 8:00 a.m. or 7:00 p.m. You may be on hold for 90 minutes if you call the MSPRC in the middle of the day.

STEP #2

When you receive the conditional payment letter from Medicare, you should try to determine what medical expenses were incurred for the injuries alleged in our client's lawsuit. For example, if our client suffered a heart attack, medical expenses relating to a knee replacement would not be related to our client's injuries in the lawsuit and therefore, they are not subject to Medicare's lien.

After you determine what medical expenses are unrelated to the injuries alleged in our client's lawsuit, you should send a letter to Medicare objecting to the unrelated medical expenses. Unless you send this letter, Medicare will assume that you agree with the amount of the Medicare lien set forth in the conditional payment letter.

This procedure will help us determine the lien amount at an early stage of the lawsuit.

STEP #3

When the case settles, you should send a final demand letter to the MSPRC. You should attach a copy of the settlement statement showing the disbursements. Only after it receives a final demand letter will the MSPRC provide you with a final lien amount.

If you do not receive a response from the MSPRC to your request for a final demand letter within 30 days, you should call the MSPRC at 1-866-677-7220 to check on the status. Upon receipt of the final demand letter from the MSPRC, you should check the Medicare payment detail to make sure that the Medicare payments were not made for unrelated medical conditions/diagnoses that were not at issue in the lawsuit.

You must make payment to Medicare as instructed in the final demand letter within 60 days to avoid interest payments at 11.25 percent.

MEDICAID LIENS

When you request a lien amount from Medicaid, you send a letter to the department of social services in the county where the Medicaid benefits have been issued. Otherwise, the procedure for getting the amount of the Medicaid lien is similar to a Medicare lien.

The Department of Social Services (DSS) will serve a notice of lien, pursuant to Section 104-b of the Social Services Law. When you receive the notice of lien, you should mail a letter to the DSS requesting a claim detail report. The claim detail report provides the services rendered, the dates of service, the diagnosis, the location where the services were rendered, and the cost of the services.

Why it's done this way: The Medicaid lien applies only to those medical expenses relating to the injuries alleged in our client's lawsuit. In a case involving blindness in one eye, the Department of Social Services is not entitled to a Medicaid lien for the expenses of a hip replacement operation. The claim detail report will allow me to determine which medical expenses are related to the injuries claimed in the lawsuit and thus reduce the amount of the Medicaid lien.

SUBROGATION CLAIMS

If a subrogation claim is asserted by a health insurance carrier, you should send a letter demanding certain documents and proof that I will need to determine if the claim has merit.

Why it's done this way: The goal is to get the lien amount as early as possible in the lawsuit. You do not want to wait until a month before trial to scramble to get the lien amount from Medicare or Medicaid. I will need the lien information before I can determine the value of the case. For example, if there is a $312k Medicare lien, our client's recovery will be significantly reduced by the lien.

One of the biggest impediments to a settlement at the time of trial is the lack of confirmation of the lien amount. To avoid this problem, *you should request the lien amount as soon as we accept the case and file the lawsuit.*

GETTING UPDATED LIEN AMOUNTS

If our client is receiving continuing medical treatment (this does not apply to wrongful death cases), you should send a request to Medicare or Medicaid for updated lien amounts at least once every six months. The lien amount will increase over the course of the lawsuit, and you should have a current lien amount once every six months.

5

MEDICAL RECORDS

The First Step in Getting Medical Records

THERE ARE TWO POWER-OF-ATTORNEY FORMS in Trialworks: a general power of attorney and an HIPAA power of attorney.

By initialing the area adjacent to the letter Q on the general power of attorney and signing it before a notary public, the client authorizes us to act on his or her behalf with regard to "insurance transactions," "claims and litigation," "records, reports, and statements," and "retirement benefit transactions," and further authorizes the attorney to delegate any or all of those powers to someone else such as a paralegal or secretary.

This allows us to have the attorney sign nearly all authorizations for nonmedical records and reports. Some situations, such as tax records, will still require a client signature.

The goal is to have all new clients sign (1) a retainer agreement, (2) a general power of attorney, and (3) an HIPAA power of attorney.

The notary public before whom the general power of attorney and/or HIPAA power of attorney is signed should *never* be the attorney named in the document.

Why it's done this way: This should allow us to obtain any and all records that we need (and to sign any and all defense authorizations) without having to waste time getting the client to sign them.

Notarizing the Client's Signature

Whenever possible, you should avoid having a client or prospective client go and find a notary public. Most people don't know what a notary public is and don't know where to find one. Having a prospective client go to another lawyer's office is somewhat counterproductive.

When we have a referring attorney whose office is near the client's home or business, you can make arrangements for the client to go to that office or have the attorney send a notary to the client. When there is no referring attorney, you should try to get the client to come to the office to meet us and sign the relevant documents or make arrangements to have someone from our office who lives closest to the client's work or home stop by to meet the client and get the necessary documents signed.

In situations in which none of the above is practical, you should locate the notary for the client, set up the appointment, and pay the notary for his/her services. The notary can be at the offices of an attorney with whom we regularly do business, or a court reporter.

During your initial communication with clients or prospective clients, you should find out if they know a notary public who could conveniently notarize documents for them.

Why it's done this way: When sending a client or prospective client off to find a notary public is one of the first acts of our relationship with our client, we are sending a message that we are not here to help but are here to make the client's life more complicated.

How to Limit the Photocopy Costs of Medical Records

If a new case is "under consideration" and I have not decided whether the case has merit, I will *never* want you to request *all* of our client's medical records. This will be very expensive, and I only need a few selected medical records to evaluate the case.

In my initial e-mail to you, I will tell you exactly which parts of our client's medical records I want and the dates of treatment. For example, my request could state, "Request the operative report, imaging reports, and discharge summary from the hospital admission between August 6 and August 8."

Why it's done this way: By limiting our request for medical records, the photocopy costs will be reduced significantly, in some cases by hundreds of dollars. This makes sense for those cases in which I am undecided whether I will accept the new case.

When You Should Mail the Requests for Medical Records

When I ask you to request certain medical records, your written request should be mailed *within 24 hours of my request*. It is not acceptable to takes days or even weeks to mail a simple request for medical records.

Why it's done this way: Our cases will not progress if it takes days or weeks to mail requests for medical records. Our clients will be calling us for answers and we will lose their case if there is nothing to report. Even if we don't have their medical records, you can at least tell our clients that their medical records were requested and explain the steps that we have taken to get the records.

Mailing Release Authorizations to Defense Counsel

As soon as you receive the initial set of discovery demands from the defense counsel, you must serve a complete set of release authorizations and medical records upon defense counsel. Do not wait to serve the release authorizations and medical records with the plaintiff's discovery responses. I want you to get the case moving with medical records and release authorizations to the defense counsel as soon as we get the initial answer and discovery demands from the defense attorneys.

Why it's done this way: The service of medical records and release authorizations upon defense counsel gets the case moving while you prepare the discovery responses and demands. By serving the records and authorizations ASAP, you remove a common excuse used by the defense counsel for adjourning depositions—namely, "We haven't had enough time to get the medical records."

Responding to Requests for New Authorizations from Defense Counsel

When you receive a request for release authorizations from defense counsel during discovery, you should provide the release authorization without asking for my permission within five (5) business days of the request.

It is okay to provide release authorizations for injuries or medical conditions that are *unrelated* to the injuries that are the subject of the lawsuit—for example, if the client sustained a brain injury and the defense lawyer requests authorizations to get our client's medical records relating to a fractured leg. I have no problem giving a release authorization to the defense lawyer for medical records relating injuries or medical conditions that are unrelated to the injuries claimed in the lawsuit.

However, there are two very important exceptions:

1. *Never* provide release authorizations for psychological or psychiatric records (unless a brain injury is the injury in the lawsuit) and

2. *Never* provide an authorization for substance abuse records, such as treatment at a drug or alcohol rehabilitation facility.

Why it's done this way: Our client's psychological and drug/alcohol records are exempt from discovery. You must object to a discovery demand that requests our client's psychological and/or drug and alcohol treatment records.

Subpoenaing Medical Records during Discovery to Limit Expenses

If the cost of getting medical records from a doctor or hospital exceeds $50, you should always serve upon the provider a subpoena duces tecum for the medical records. The subpoena duces tecum will direct the production of a certified copy of the medical records to our law office. (Note: You should always make sure you send a copy of the subpoena duces tecum to defense counsel, as required by Article 23 of the CPLR).

You should never send a release authorization with a written request for medical records when the records exceed 100 pages. Subpoenaing the medical records saves our client a lot of money with large medical records.

Why it's done this way: When you subpoena medical records (see CPLR Section 3122-a for legal authority), the medical provider is entitled to a subpoena fee ($15) and a small mileage fee. The most the medical provider can charge rarely exceeds $50. Although they will try, the medical recorders cannot charge a photocopy fee (75 cents per page), when we subpoena the medical records. If the medical records consist of more than 100 pages, it always makes sense to subpoena the records instead of sending a release authorization. This will save our firm and our client a lot of money.

The medical provider will often try to charge the photocopy fee when you subpoena the medical records, but this is not permissible under the law. When you get an invoice for a photocopy fee after you subpoena medical records, you should mail a letter to the medical provider, or photocopy service, stating that the photocopy fees are impermissible and you assume this was an oversight on his/her part. Whatever you do, *make sure you do not pay the photocopy fee when you subpoena medical records.*

When you receive the certified medical records from the medical provider, you should send a letter to the defense counsel informing him/her that you received the medical records and they are available for copying and inspection by the defense counsel. If you do not notify the defense counsel of your receipt of the medical records, I will not be able to enter the records into evidence at the trial (see CPLR Section 3122-a).

Inspecting and Scanning the Original Medical Records

We must *always* require the production of the original medical records and scan the records in color.

Why it's done this way: The worst thing in the world for me is to be confronted with medical records that I have never seen before at the deposition of the defendant. This really drives me batty (and it's really bad for our client's case). The only way to make sure this does not happen is to insist that the defense lawyer gives us an opportunity to inspect the original medical records and scan the original records in color with a laser color scanner.

After the original medical records have been scanned in color, the complete medical records should be sent to our medical experts, as they request, either on a compact disc, hard copy, or a file-sharing website (e.g., www.dropbox.com).

The website www.dropbox.com offers a free service that lets you share all of our photographs, documents, and videos with experts anywhere. If you want our experts to have access to a file, you can upload the file documents and send an e-mail to the expert granting access to the records from any web browser. It's as though you had saved the file to the expert's computer. Dropbox is a great way to quickly and cheaply share file materials with our experts.

Follow Up with Requests for Medical Records

After you send a request for medical records, it is your job to make sure we have the medical records within twenty one days. The doctors and hospitals will ignore the statutory 10-day deadline set forth in Section 18 of the Public Health Law. It is your job to follow up with the doctors and hospitals to make sure we get the medical records within 21 days.

If you mail requests for medical records, your job is not done. If you do not possess the medical records within ten business days of your request, you should call the medical provider to ask why you don't have the medical records and follow up with a fax to confirm your telephone conversation. If you don't keep on top of the medical providers, it may take as long as two or three months (or longer) to get the medical records.

What You Should Do after You Receive the Power of Attorney from Our Client

When you receive the power of attorney signed and notarized from our client, *DO NOT file the power of attorney. Wait for instructions from me.*

On the same day that you receive the fully signed and notarized power of attorney from the client, you should:

- Check the Memorandum tab in Trialworks to determine if I specified the medical records that I need in order to evaluate the case. If there is a memo under the Memorandum tab of Trialworks, mail a letter for the medical records that are specified in the memo.

- If there is no memorandum specifying the medical records that I need, you should send an e-mail to me that reads, "Today we received the power of attorney from our client. What medical records do you want to request?" I will respond with an e-mail that specifies the medical records that I want.

Once you know which medical records I need for the case, your request for the medical records should be mailed within 24 hours, and preferably on the same day that you receive instructions as to which records to request.

Why it's done this way: The last thing we want is a power of attorney just sitting in Trialworks without a request for medical records. The medical records should be requested on the same day that we receive the power of attorney from our client. If you do not request the medical records as soon as we receive the power of attorney, this will just prolong the time that it takes for us to get the medical records. Our client deserves better.

What You Should Do When You Receive the Medical Records

After you scan the medical records and send them to the appropriate case file in Trialworks, you should review the records to make sure the medical provider gave you all of the medical records that were requested. Even when you request the complete medical records for all dates of treatment, it is common for medical providers to give you an incomplete set of the medical records. *You should NEVER assume that the medical providers will send a complete set of the medical records.* They usually don't.

If you determine that we have an incomplete set of medical records, you should call the medical provider to request *all* of the medical records and confirm the phone conversation with a letter.

It is your job to make sure we get all of the medical records that have been requested.

What You Should Do with Medical Records Provided by Our Clients

In many cases, clients with potential cases provide us with their medical records. When we get the medical records from our clients, you should scan the medical records under the Medical Records tab of Trialworks and then call the clients to ask if they want the medical records back.

If our clients want us to return their medical records, you should mail the records to them. If our clients do not want the medical records, you should shred the medical records in order to protect our clients' privacy rights.

Why it's done this way: When I reject potential cases, our clients will almost always want their medical records returned to them and there's a good reason: they want to shop for a new lawyer. That's their right, and it's your job to make sure they get their medical records back from us.

Authenticating Medical Records for Trial

You should ensure that the compact disc of medical records is authenticated before trial by serving a copy of it, with our notice to admit, on defense counsel. You must serve the notice to admit with the compact disc of medical records at least 30 days before the first day of the trial.

You should prepare a letter to the defense counsel that lists every medical record and nonmedical record that we intend to admit into evidence at the trial, together with a compact disc of the records, and request a response from the defense counsel as to whether he/she will stipulate into evidence the records. You should place a deadline for a response from the defense counsel.

If the defense lawyer will not agree to stipulate the medical records into evidence, you should call the Supreme Court clerk's office to schedule a time to review the subpoenaed records at the clerk's office. You should review the subpoenaed records during the week before the first day of the trial. When you review the subpoenaed records at the Supreme Court clerk's office, you should prepare a checklist of the records that have been produced to the clerk and whether they are properly certified and what records have not been produced pursuant to your subpoena duces tecum.

You should e-mail a memo to me that lists every record that has been produced, whether it is certified or not, and which records have not been produced. You should place phone calls to the medical providers who did not provide records pursuant to our subpoena or whose records were not properly certified. You should inform the medical providers that the medical records must be produced with a certification at 9:00 a.m. at the Supreme Court clerk's office on the first day of the trial. If you encounter any problems with the medical providers, you should send an e-mail to me.

The goal is to have all medical records and business records stipulated into evidence by the defense counsel before the first day of the trial. This relieves one more thing that I have to think about at the trial.

Why it's done this way: If there will be a problem getting medical records admitted into evidence at the trial, you should find out before the first day of the trial. The last thing I need is to show up on the first day of the trial to discover that the defense attorney has objections to the medical records due to the absence of a certification from the medical records custodian.

Authenticating Imaging Films for Trial

Under the Pleadings tab in Trialworks there are "Notice to Introduce Evidence & Affirmation," and "Physician's Affirmation Regarding Films and Tests" forms. These are designed to take full advantage of our ability to offer X-rays and the results of other diagnostic tests, including MRI, CT scans and fetal heart tracings, at trial, without producing a live witness.

The procedure is set forth in CPLR Section 4532-a and requires that the X-ray or test is inscribed with the required information and that it is attested by a physician. The notice and affirmation must be served at least 10 days before trial (add five extra days if serving by mail) and the X-ray or test must be available for inspection but need not accompany the notice.

This process is only going to be useful if you get the affirmation signed by the physician well in advance of the time to serve the notice.

Why it's done this way: This saves the time spent getting a radiologist to testify at the trial about an imaging study in order to get the test in evidence at the trial.

Release Authorizations Provided to Defendant's Attorneys

You should never use a release authorization issued by the NYS Department of Health (as defense counsel will often insist that you do). You should only use the release authorizations and Arons authorizations used by me.

Defendants' lawyers will send you release authorizations on standard preprinted forms (Office of Court Administration form 960) issued by the New York State Department of Health (DOH). The preprinted forms "approved" by the DOH for the release of medical records and ex parte interviews between defense counsel and the plaintiff's treating physicians *should never be used.*

The DOH release authorizations provide none of the safeguards against the accidental (or intentional) disclosure of privileged medical information and treating physicians may mistakenly think that a private, ex parte meeting with the defendant's counsel is mandatory.

The DOH release authorizations do not contain any of the *warnings* that are permitted for release authorizations issued to defendants' attorneys. Pursuant to *Porcelli v. Northern Westchester Hospital Center*, 65 A.D.3d 176 (2nd Dep't 2009), the release authorizations are permitted to provide the following warnings:

- "The purpose of the requested interview with the physician is solely to assist defense counsel at trial."

- "The physician is not obligated to speak with defense counsel prior to trial. The interview is voluntary."

In addition to the warnings on the release authorizations, plaintiff's counsel is permitted to put the warning in boldface type and emphasize the warning in red with yellow highlighting. Consistent with the holding in Porcelli, we place yellow highlighting over the warnings and add a third warning to the release authorizations provided to the defendants' attorneys:

- "Any discussion with defense counsel is entirely voluntary and MUST BE LIMITED IN SCOPE to the particular medical condition at issue in the litigation."

In order to make sure that the defendants' attorneys use the color version of our Arons release authorization, our authorization includes a statement that:

- "This authorization is VOID if the above NOTICE is not highlighted in YELLOW."

You should object *immediately*, as soon as you receive the release authorizations provided by the defendants' attorneys on the pre-printed forms issued by the New York State Department of Health.

Why it's done this way: The DOH release authorizations contain no warnings or information regarding the voluntary nature of the interview between defendants' attorneys and the treating physicians or the purpose of the interview. With the DOH release authorizations in hand, the defendants' attorneys can meet with plaintiffs' treating physicians under the guise that such a meeting is mandatory and there is no topic that is off limits. In order to prevent the accidental disclosure of privileged medical information, you must *only* provide defendants' attorneys with release authorizations that we prepare. *Never* provide the DOH release authorizations.

Warning Letters to Treating Physicians Regarding Meetings with Defendant's Attorneys

In addition to the warnings on the Arons authorizations, you should send a letter to the plaintiff's treating physicians to alert them that our client prefers that they do not meet with defendant's attorneys and that if they decide to meet with them, I would like to attend the meeting.

Updating Medical Records

At least once every four to six weeks, you should call our clients to ask if they have had any recent medical treatment since you last spoke to them and you should find out whether you need to send a written request for updated medical records.

As you receive updated medical records, you should mail the new records to defense counsel in a digital format—namely, a compact disc or pdf, as opposed to a paper format. Your cover letter to the defense counsel should specify the name of the provider and the dates of treatment for the new medical records.

Why it's done this way: If you do not send the updated medical records to the defense counsel, the court will not permit me to use the new medical records at the trial. Please send the updated medical records to the defense counsel *without* asking for my permission.

Mailing Medical Records to Expert Witnesses

You should send medical records to experts on a compact disc unless experts insist on paper records. Your initial letter to experts should state that we are asking for their "professional, objective and independent opinion" and identify the list of medical records by the names of the medical providers.

Some of our computer-savvy experts will agree to review medical records through a file-sharing website such as www.dropbox.com. File-sharing websites are a quick and easy way to share voluminous medical records with medical experts. You should ask experts if they prefer to get the medical records on a compact disc or a hard copy, or review the records on a file-sharing website. Whatever the medical experts prefer is fine with me.

After you send the medical records to the experts, you should e-mail or call them to schedule a date for me to speak with them by phone. I will usually only need 15–20 minutes to speak with them by phone. You should enter the phone conference in Microsoft Outlook and notify me with an e-mail about the appointment.

Records to send to Expert Witnesses

While it makes sense to orally tell an expert what documents she might want to focus on, it is never appropriate to send her anything short of ALL the available documents that are relevant to her testimony.

The expert should receive: the complete underlying file; all pleadings and discovery in the case; expert responses, DME reports, bills of particulars, all depositions of all persons in the case; any other materials which might be relevant. You should keep an itemized list of what was sent to the expert, so we can make certain that any expert who may be asked to testify on any of the same or related issues will receive identical materials.

Why it's done this way: If you do not send all of the documents relevant to the expert's testimony, the expert will be subject to a devastating cross-examination in which defense counsel makes it appear that the plaintiff's attorney is using the expert as a puppet to espouse the theories developed by the plaintiff's attorney and then sent the material to support that theory.

Do NOT Request Medical Bills until I Decide to Accept the Case

Unless I have accepted the case—namely, we will file the lawsuit and have the client sign a retainer agreement—you should *never* request medical bills. In order to evaluate a new case, I do not need any of the medical bills/invoices, so you should not request them.

When I tell you that we will accept a new case and file the lawsuit, only then should you request the medical billing records.

Why it's done this way: It is a complete waste of our money to request medical bills on potential cases. I reject 98 percent of new cases and it makes no sense to request medical bills that I don't need to determine whether the new case has merit.

The "Records Retention Policy"

There is no need to keep paper records, with the exception of court orders, affidavits, and witness statements. As long as all documents are scanned and stored in a digital format, there is no need to keep a hard file.

Why it's done this way: You should treat our clients' medical records with respect. Medical records that are to be disposed of should be shredded to protect "private" material that is contained therein. If you have any doubt, shred it (see Department of Defense, Top Secret Document Shredding, Level 6).

Storage of Imaging Films (MRIs, CT scans, and X-rays)

You should request that medical providers give us a copy of imaging studies (MRIs, CT scans, and X-rays) on a compact disc. When you receive the compact disc of the imaging films, you should upload the images into the client's case file under the Miscellaneous tab of Trialworks.

If the medical provider cannot provide the imaging films on a compact disc and can only provide a hard copy of the imaging films, you must keep a separate manila file of the imaging films with the name of the client identified in big, bold letters on the file. The manila file should be stored in a filing cabinet in the office that is used only for the storage of imaging films.

You should always keep in mind that medical providers often send us the originals of the imaging films, even though we only request a copy of the films. If the medical provider sends the originals of the imaging films to us and the films are misplaced or lost within our office, you may not be able to get another copy from the medical provider.

What Do You Do if Clients Request Their Files?

The files belong to the clients. You should make certain that you have complete scanned copies of files. Nothing should be given to the clients that you don't have a copy of.

After you burn the clients' files to a compact disc, you can mail the compact discs to the clients as long as they sign a receipt acknowledging that a copy of the file was sent to them. The clients' receipts for the files should be filed under the Miscellaneous tab of Trialworks and notations should be made under the Notes tab of Trialworks, stating the dates when files were given to the clients.

Why it's done this way: The New York Court of Appeals has determined that materials in client files properly belong to the clients rather than the attorneys: *Sage Realty Corp. v. Proskauer Rose Goetz*, 91 N.Y.2d 30, 689 N.E.2d 879, 666 N.Y.S.2d 985 (1997).

6

DEPOSITIONS

IN EVERY LAWSUIT there are typically a minimum of four (4) to five (5) depositions and usually a maximum of ten (10) to twelve (12) depositions. The persons to be deposed in every case consist of three parties: (1) plaintiffs, (2) defendants, and (3) nonparty witnesses.

In personal injury and medical malpractice lawsuits in New York, there are deadlines imposed by the court for the scheduling of depositions in a court order known as a preliminary conference stipulation and order. Typically, the preliminary conference stipulation and order will contain an "outside deadline" for the completion of all depositions. *It is very important to schedule the depositions before the deadline set forth in the preliminary conference stipulation and order.*

In most cases, the deadline for the completion of all depositions is six months from the date of the first preliminary court conference, at which the attorneys meet to discuss deadlines for the completion of all aspects of discovery—namely, discovery demands and responses and depositions. Thus, in most cases, you will have six months to schedule the depositions of all parties and nonparty witnesses after you have been given the assignment to schedule depositions.

There are three basic steps to scheduling a deposition:

Scheduling the Deposition

After you serve the plaintiff's discovery responses, you should contact the defense counsel by phone to schedule deposition dates of all parties. If the defense counsel does not call you back within 48 hours, you must call him/her. You should never assume that defense counsel will cooperate in scheduling depositions; they almost never do.

You are solely responsible for scheduling depositions. I do not schedule depositions.

You should make phone calls to the attorneys representing the defendants in order to schedule dates for the depositions. In almost all cases, you will ask to speak with the "deposition clerk" or the secretary to the defendant's attorney.

You will inform the defendant's deposition clerk that you are calling to schedule dates for the depositions of the plaintiff, defendant, and in some cases, nonparty witnesses, and he/she will ask for alternative dates when the defendant's attorneys are available for the depositions.

You must coordinate a date for the depositions of the plaintiffs, defendants, and nonparty witnesses that is acceptable to the defendant's attorneys. Typically, you will ask the defendant's deposition clerk for multiple dates when the defendant's attorney is available for the depositions.

It is common and should be expected that defendants' deposition clerks will *not* cooperate with the deposition scheduler. It often takes multiple phone calls to confirm a date for a single deposition. It does not suffice to make a single phone call, leave a voice message, and expect the defendant's deposition clerk to respond. Defendants' deposition clerks rarely cooperate. Persistence is crucial when it comes to scheduling depositions with defendants' deposition clerks.

Confirming the Deposition

Once you have multiple dates when all of the attorneys are available for the depositions, you will confirm the dates for the depositions with a letter to the defendant's attorneys.

The letter to the defendant's attorneys will state the time, date, and location of the deposition and who will be paying the stenographer's fee for the deposition:

> This confirms that we have confirmed Monday, December 3, 2012, as the date for the plaintiff's depositions at Valley Reporting Service at 115 Green Street in Kingston, New York, at 10:00 a.m. The defendant's counsel will provide the stenographer for the plaintiff's depositions.

Once a date for the deposition has been confirmed with a letter to the defendant's counsel, you should enter the date in the Master Calendar in Microsoft Outlook and inform me by e-mail of the date for the depositions.

Reconfirming the Deposition

One day before the deposition, you should call the defendant's attorneys to confirm the deposition—namely: "I am calling to confirm the deposition of the plaintiff, Mr. Jones, tomorrow at 10:00 a.m. at Valley Reporting in Kingston." Once the deposition has been reconfirmed on the day before the deposition, the deposition scheduler should send an e-mail to the assigned attorney stating, "Tomorrow's deposition of Mr. Jones has been confirmed with the defendant's counsel."

Make Sure We Have a Complete Set of Discovery Responses from the Defense before Scheduling Depositions

You should never schedule the depositions of the defendants *until* you confirm that we have received a complete set of discovery responses from the defense attorneys.

Before you schedule the defendant's depositions, please check the Discovery tab in Trialworks to determine whether we received the defendant's discovery responses and, if so, make sure the defense lawyer provided us with actual documents in response to the plaintiff's discovery demand.

Warning! Defense counsel will often serve a discovery response that reads, "Defendants will provide the requested documents at a future date." This is *not* a discovery response. My translation of such a response is: "We are too busy to respond to the plaintiff's combined discovery demands and we'll get the requested documents to you when we feel like it." If the defense attorneys serve a nonsense discovery response like this, it is your job to remind them *before the depositions are scheduled* that we are entitled to a real response that provides the documents that we requested, such as the hospital's policies and procedures.

If we do not possess a complete set of medical records from the defense attorneys before the defendant's depositions, I will adjourn the depositions until we have the defendant's discovery responses. *It is your job to make sure that doesn't happen.*

Why it's done this way: I cannot prepare for a deposition of a key physician or nurse without a complete set of discovery responses from the defendant's counsel. It is your job to make sure that the defense attorneys have provided us with a complete set of meaningful discovery responses before you schedule the defendant's depositions.

Depositions of Nonparty Witnesses

When I ask you to subpoena a nonparty witness for a deposition, you should always have the witness *personally* served with a subpoena. *Do NOT serve the subpoena by mail.* You should hire a process server to serve the subpoena upon the nonparty witness.

Why it's done this way: If you attempt to serve subpoenas upon the nonparty witnesses by mail, they will ignore the subpoena 90 percent of the time. If the witnesses ignore the subpoena, I will not be able to make a motion to hold the witnesses in contempt since they never accepted service of the subpoena. Let's make things simple by personally serving the subpoena upon the nonparty witnesses.

Getting Alternative Dates for Depositions *before* the First Preliminary Conference

You should send a letter to defense counsel stating:

Counselors:

In an effort to establish a mutually agreeable timetable for the completion of all disclosure proceedings in this case, please provide the undersigned, within 20 days of the date of this letter, with five (5) or more specific dates between now and (enter a date approximately three months from the date of the defendant's answer) when your clients will be available to give their depositions upon oral examination in this action.

In addition to your clients, please provide the same information regarding the following individuals, who I believe are current employees of your clients: (insert name of witness).

Upon receipt of your response to this request, we will proceed to schedule the depositions of such individuals.

If we do not receive a response to this request, we will proceed to schedule the depositions of such individuals.

If we do not receive a response to our request within 20 days, we will select deposition dates that are convenient for the plaintiffs and will request that the court enter an order directing that the depositions be conducted on those dates.

We look forward to your anticipated cooperation in setting mutually agreeable deposition dates that are convenient for all parties and their counsel.

Very truly yours,

How to Deal with Difficult Defense Counsel

Follow-up with defense counsel in scheduling depositions is a crucial part of your job. When you call defense counsel to schedule a deposition, your job is not done. The scheduling of a deposition is complete only after you confirm a date for the deposition with defense counsel and confirm the deposition in writing with details of the date, time, location, and names of the stenographer and videographer.

If the defense counsel is not cooperating with you, you must call the defense counsel as many times as necessary to confirm a date for the depositions. Until you have a date confirmed for all depositions with the defense counsel, you must keep calling the defense counsel.

If you do not have dates for the depositions of all parties within ten business days of the dates you served the plaintiff's discovery responses, you should prepare a letter to the court informing the judge of the defense counsel's lack of cooperation and asking the judge to impose "so-ordered" specific dates for all of the depositions.

Scheduling Phone Conferences with Medical Experts *before* the Deposition

When you schedule dates for the deposition of the "target" defendant in a medical malpractice case (the "target defendant" is typically the first named defendant in the caption of the lawsuit), you should contact our medical expert/physician to schedule a date for a phone conference with the "target" defendant *at least three days before the deposition.*

You should explain to our medical experts that I will want to discuss with them the questions that should be asked at the deposition and the answers that they expect from the defendant. You should tell our medical experts that I will need about one hour for such phone conferences.

Why it's done this way: A big part of my preparation for the deposition of a "target" defendant is a phone conference with my medical expert. I need to make sure I leave no rock unturned at the deposition and the only way to make sure that happens is a phone conference with the medical expert.

When I was less experienced, I didn't meet or have phone conferences with medical experts before depositions. Then, inevitably, the medical expert would review the deposition transcript and call me asking why I didn't ask the most important questions. The phone conference with the medical expert is my way of making sure that doesn't happen.

Original Chart Review Must Be Done *at Least One Week* before the Defendant's Deposition

It is your job to make sure that a date is scheduled with the defense lawyers for an original chart review *at least one week* before the defendant's depositions. An original chart review is an appointment that you schedule with the defense lawyer at which I will inspect the original medical records at the defense lawyer's office or the defendant's medical office.

The location of the original chart review is unimportant—defense lawyer's office or the defendant's medical office—I will agree to review the original medical records anywhere. What is important is that I review the original medical records, compare the original medical records to the medical records that we possess, and make sure that we are not missing any records.

It is absolutely essential that I conduct an original chart review at least one week before the defendant's depositions. If defense lawyers say no to an original chart review, you should remind them that Section 18 of the Public Health Law gives our client the right to inspect the original medical records.

If the defense lawyers still say no, you should contact the assigned judge's clerk or secretary to ask for a telephone conference to address this discovery dispute. Trust me, the defense lawyers don't have a leg to stand on. Once you request a telephone conference with the judge, the defense lawyers will back off and grudgingly allow the original chart review.

Why it's done this way: I do not want to arrive at the defendant's deposition and find new medical records (that I have never seen before). If that happens, I will not be able to conduct an effective deposition for two reasons: (a) I will not have time to evaluate the new records and questions that might flow from them (I don't like "winging it" when a severely disabled client's rights are at stake), and (b) my medical experts will not have reviewed the new medical records and, hence, I will not have the benefit of their analysis of the records.

How You Should Make Sure the Defense Discloses Electronic Records at the Original Chart Review

Once you confirm a date with defense counsel for an original chart review, you should send a letter confirming the date and time of the original chart review. In your letter, you should specify that, in addition to the paper copies of the medical records, hard copies of all electronic records will be produced.

If you don't specifically demand the production of paper copies of all electronic records, the electronic records will not be produced at the original chart review.

At least two days before the original chart review, you should call the defense counsel to confirm that paper copies of all electronic records will be available for inspection at the original chart review. If you do not get confirmation from the defense counsel, you should tell him/her that you will reschedule the original chart review once he/she can confirm that paper copies of all electronic records will also be available for inspection.

Why it's done this way: Most medical practices use electronically stored information, including e-mails, billing, and calendar appointments. E-mails, in particular, may be crucial to evaluating the case and without the electronic records, a complete understanding of the medical records is impossible.

What to Do When the Defense Lawyer Postpones Depositions

Defense lawyers will not schedule the depositions of the parties until after they get all of the medical records, even if that means violating a court order for the completion of depositions.

So, what do you do when the defense lawyers claim they do not have all of our client's medical records? First, you make sure the defense lawyers are correct (they usually have no idea what medical records they possess). You should check the correspondence to determine which medical records and release authorizations you have already mailed to the defense lawyers. There's a good chance the defense lawyers already have a complete set of medical records.

If you have already mailed a complete set of medical records and release authorizations to the defense lawyers, you should call the defense lawyers and state, "Our records indicate that you received a complete set of medical records and release authorizations on March 1. Are there any other records you do not have?" After fumbling for a response, the defense lawyer's secretary will usually agree to schedule dates for the depositions.

Video Depositions

You must videotape every deposition unless there is a specific instruction not to do so. All depositions (with the exception of the plaintiffs/our clients) in all cases should be noticed or cross-noticed to be done on videotape unless there is a specific written instruction from the attorney who will be doing the deposition, stating that a specific deposition is not to be done on videotape.

The depositions of our clients (the plaintiffs) are never videotaped.

Such written instruction shall be given before the notice is signed and the attorney's specific reason for not wanting to videotape the deposition is stated in the memo. Thus, the "default mode" for all depositions noticed or cross-noticed is that they are to be done on videotape.

You must make sure that you have scheduled a videographer and stenographer for the depositions.

Why it's done this way: Videotape depositions are 10 times more powerful than nonvideotape depositions. The facial expressions, verbal pauses, and mannerisms while answering questions are not picked up by the stenographer, but on video they are pure gold. Cases can be won or lost depending on whether a deposition is videotaped. So, I videotape all depositions, with the exception of our clients' depositions.

Original Medical Records at the Deposition

For all depositions of defendants in medical malpractice cases, I always want the original records (e.g., hospital chart or office chart) present at the deposition. If you don't ask the defense counsel to bring the original chart to the deposition, I will have not the original chart at the deposition.

At least two days before the defendant's deposition, you should confirm with the defendant's counsel that he/she will bring the original medical records to the deposition. When you have confirmation from the defense counsel, you should send me an e-mail stating, "Mr. Jones, counsel for the defendant, will have the original hospital chart at tomorrow's deposition."

Why it's done this way: *A copy of the medical records is not the same as the original chart.* The original medical records will usually be more complete than our copy of the medical records and they often contain billing records, scripts, and documentation of phone calls that were not disclosed by the defendants in their discovery responses. The only way of guaranteeing that I have a complete set of the medical records is to insist that the defendant's counsel produce the original medical records at the defendant's depositions.

EBT Transcript to Request from Stenographer

You must make sure that you request in writing that the videotaped portion is provided to me on a DVD. In addition, please make certain that there is a written request to the stenographer that we receive the transcript in an ASC-II format, either on disc or by e-mail. This will allow me to "synch" the video testimony with the transcript, allowing all or portions of the video of the deposition to be played while the transcript of the testimony being seen appears on the screen simultaneously.

EBT Transcripts to Expert Witnesses

When all of the deposition transcripts have been received, you should put them on a compact disc and mail the CD to our expert witnesses. In the cover letter that accompanies the CD, you should list each EBT transcript by the name of the witness. This will ensure that our experts have all of the deposition transcripts.

Why it's done this way: It always happens. As I am one week away from trial, I meet with my crucial expert witness, and we review the file records that I mailed to him. To my horror, I discover that the expert does not possess critical deposition transcripts that might have a big impact on his/her trial testimony. To avoid this horror story, you should make sure we send all of the deposition transcripts to our experts.

After all of the depositions have been completed, you should send a letter or e-mail to the expert that lists every deposition transcript in the case and ask him/her to confirm that he/she possesses all of the transcripts.

Documents to Send Clients *before* Their Deposition

You should mail the plaintiffs' bill of particulars to our clients one week before their deposition and ask them to review their bill of particulars in preparation for their deposition. The plaintiff's bill of particulars is the only document you should ask our clients to review before their deposition.

Why it's done this way: I want our clients to be familiar with their bill of particulars. Oftentimes, our clients will spot information that is either incorrect or incomplete in their bill of particulars and that helps us make corrections and improvements to their bill of particulars.

Schedule Meeting with Client to Prepare for Deposition

Once you confirm dates for our clients' depositions with the defense counsels, you should call our clients to schedule an appointment for me to meet with them one week before their deposition. I do not want to meet with clients on the morning of their deposition or the night before the deposition. You can schedule this meeting at our clients' homes or my office, whichever the clients prefer.

You should inform our clients that I will need two hours to meet with them for the initial meeting to prepare for their deposition, and that I will also need to meet with them 45 minutes before their deposition for a final meeting. If any clients do not want to spend the time preparing for their deposition, you should let me know; it may be time to fire them.

Why it's done this way: I need to find out if there is a major problem—for example, the client spent time in a Mexican jail for armed robbery and murder—at least one week before the deposition. I do not want to find out about a major problem the day of the deposition or the night before. This is why I need to meet with the clients one week before their deposition.

Location of the Defendants' Depositions

Unless I agree otherwise, the depositions of the defendants should always be held at our law office. We have the right to decide the location of the defendants' depositions and it is almost always my preference to conduct the defendants' depositions at our law office.

The defense lawyer will almost always try to convince you to hold the defendant's deposition at his law office, the doctor's office, or the hospital. That is not acceptable to me. Since I get to decide where the deposition of the defendant will be held, you should schedule a defendant's deposition at our law office.

Location of Depositions of Nonparty Witnesses

Nonparty witnesses can only be deposed in the county where they reside or have their primary place of business (see CPLR Section 3110). Hence, the depositions of nonparty witnesses can only be held at our law office if the nonparty witness resides or works in Ulster County.

If the nonparty witness resides or works outside Ulster County, you should call a stenographer service for the location of a deposition suite where the deposition can be held in that county. Most stenographer services provide a deposition suite as part of their service. If the stenographers cannot provide a deposition suite at their office, you should ask me for the name of a law firm in the town where the deposition will be held and you can call the firm to ask if we can use its conference room for the deposition.

7

PAPERLESS OFFICE AND SCANNING

Scanning

THE FOLLOWING ARE *rules* (not things you should do only if you have time):

Scan all documents and e-mail them to the assigned attorney *on the day when they first arrive in the office.* No letter, pleading, bill, report, medical record or any other material that belongs in a file in this office is ever to be delivered to a lawyer or put in a file until it has first been scanned into the correct file and e-mailed to the lawyer who should receive it. The goal is to scan everything and photocopy as little as possible.

Scanning of incoming mail takes priority over everything else. The mail must be scanned, transferred to Trialworks, and e-mailed to the attorney before anything else is done.

If any attorneys have something that needs to be completed and the secretary is busy scanning, transferring, and e-mailing the day's mail, the attorneys must do for themselves and not interrupt the secretary.

Under no circumstances should anyone leave the office for the day without having fulfilled these obligations.

All documents (medical records, pleadings, correspondence, bills, etc.) must be scanned into Trialworks. Every letter, pleading, bill, report, medical record, and any other material that is received in this office that relates to a current or potential file shall be immediately scanned into the correct file and delivered by e-mail to the lawyer who is responsible for it *on the same day* that it arrives in the office. The responsibility for scanning medical records will fall upon the secretaries.

Every incoming fax should go to the secretary who will scan and e-mail it to the assigned attorney.

If a letter or document is received by fax and scanned into Trialworks, the next day, when a hard copy of the letter comes in the mail, it does not get rescanned.

If a fax arrives in the evening after the staff has left for the day, the attorney to whom the fax is addressed may make a copy of the fax and leave the original fax for the secretary to scan into Trialworks the next day.

With the use of appropriate software (Adobe Acrobat), medical records, and other documents can be instantaneously searched for specific words or phrases and can be automatically numbered and indexed.

You must make certain that your backup system is absolutely infallible.

Why it's done this way: The goal is to eliminate the time spent trying to find materials in files and the hours of copying that occur when materials need to be sent to experts. It will also be much easier for lawyers who want to access the complete contents of a file from home or a remote location. It will also allow us to send documents and records to experts as e-mail attachments or on recordable compact discs.

This will eliminate the need to carry bulky files to court, conferences, or depositions. This will also facilitate the storage of closed files and the retrieval of information from those files in the future.

How to Scan Documents

File-It is the heart of scanning.

1. Scan the document to a network location, for example, the S drive.

2. Each user should have his/her own directory.

3. The person who is doing the scanning scans the documents into his/her own directory.

4. Once all documents are scanned in, click on File-It and fill in the information concerning which file, which tab in the file, the file name, and the description each document is to be given;

5. Once File-It is complete, hit "transfer files," and all of the files are transferred to Trialworks. This is a "cut and paste," so nothing is left in the user's directory. This prevents having duplicated documents in the system and lets users know whether they have transferred everything that they have scanned in.

Where to Scan Documents

The Correspondence tab should contain the following:

- All incoming and outgoing correspondence

The Pleadings tab should contain the following:

- Summons and Complaint

- Amended Complaint

- Answer

- Amended Answer

- Third Party Summons and Complaint

- Demands for Verified Bills of Particulars

- Verified Bills of Particulars

- Stipulation Discontinuing Action; Judgments

- Notice of Claim

- Notice of Intention to File Claim

- Supplemental Demand for Damages

- Cross Claims

- Notice of Commencement of Medical Malpractice Action

- Demand for Damage

- Response to Demand for Damages

- Consent to Change Attorney

- Bill of Costs

- Preliminary Conference Stipulation and Order

- So-Ordered letters

- Request for Judicial Intervention

The summons and complaint are sent to the county clerk's office for filing. When the time stamped copy is returned, that copy is scanned in as "pleading additional" alongside the originally created summons and complaint.

Appeals should be placed under the Appeals tab.

The Discovery tab should contain the following:

- Notice rescinding service by fax (if done in the form of a pleading; if done by letter, place under the Correspondence tab)

- Demands for Discovery

- Responses to Discovery Demands

- Notice to Admit

- Response to Notice to Admit

- Subpoenas served on us by other parties

- Policies and procedures produced by defense

- Rule 26 Disclosure (in federal court cases)

In Federal Court cases when you get an electronic notification of the filing of a document, the electronic notification gets scanned under the tab where the document it relates to has been scanned. For example, if you get an electronic notification of the defense filing the answer, the electronic notification and the answer would both be scanned under the Pleadings tab.

The Deposition tab should contain the following:

- Deposition notices

- Deposition transcripts

- Deposition exhibits

All subpoenas should be created under the Subpoena tab.
Medical Records tab:

- All medical records should be created under this tab.

Except copies of medical records received in our office from the defense, which the defense has obtained with an authorization that we provided, medical records get scanned under the Medical Record tab and are to be reviewed by either the attorney or paralegal, who will compare it to the record we received with our request and authorization, and a determination will be made by the attorney or paralegal as to whether any, all, or a portion of the record will be entered under the Production Tracker tab.

Research tab:

- All research must be put under this tab. Either save from Westlaw to Word or Adobe file and put it under this tab.

Production Tracker tab:

- This tab should contain trial exhibits only.

What to Do with the Paper Copies after Scanning into Trialworks

You should simply scan the originals of all documents and keep them in a digital format instead of keeping paper copies. The fact that the letter or discovery demand was signed will serve as an indication to me that it was sent to the client or defense counsel.

The basic concept is to scan everything that we can and to photocopy as little as possible.

It is important to treat patients' and clients' medical records with respect. Medical records that are to be disposed of should be shredded to protect the "private" material that is contained therein. I use the word "private" rather than "confidential" because the "confidentiality" of the records has almost certainly been waived.

With regard to deposition transcripts, there was never any confidentiality in the first instance because the deposition was not taken under any circumstances that would give rise to an expectation of confidentiality. If a deposition transcript is going to be discarded, it should be shredded to protect the "privacy" issues of the patient. By shredding all documents and records that are being discarded, you save the time and effort involved in sorting the private from the nonprivate materials.

Why it's done this way: Rather than HIPAA, the real concern in handling medical records relates to identity theft and potential liability for negligently disposing of records in such a manner that facilitates the theft of the client's/patient's identity. My policy regarding the shredding of "sensitive material" is that any material that contains confidential or medical information or any information that could be used to facilitate identity theft of anyone is to be shredded. *If you have any doubt, shred it!*

Shredding

The shredder is to be used for shredding all confidential documents and medical records. The shredder should be used on a daily basis whenever medical records, pleadings, or information that identifies any person is being thrown out. This should include any material that has anyone's Social Security number, employer identification number, date of birth, or other identifying information on it that could be used for identity theft.

You should segregate paper that needs to be shredded and dispose of it at the end of the day.

Why it's done this way: Our clients and other individuals with whom we do business are entitled to expect that the personal information that they provide to us will be safeguarded. You can figure out what needs to be shredded and what doesn't. If you have any doubt, shred it!

Federal Court Electronic Notification

When we receive the electronic notification of the filing of any document in federal court, the following procedure should be followed:

- Print a copy of the notification and attached document;

- Save the notification and attached document in the S drive so the documents can be transferred via File-It under the appropriate tab in Trialworks;

- E-mail the document to the attorney and paralegal.

If an attorney or paralegal receiving notification of an electronic filing find it necessary that they have to open the attached document, it is that attorney's or paralegal's responsibility to either save the document in the appropriate drive so it can be moved to Trialworks or make a copy of the document so it can be scanned into Trialworks by the secretary.

We are allowed to open an electronically filed document only once without incurring a charge. After that we must pay a fee.

During the course of a normal business day, there should be no need for the attorney or paralegal to open the electronically filed document as it only takes the secretary a few minutes to open the electronically filed document, copy it, and save it to the S drive and move it via File-It under the correct tab in Trialworks.

8

TRIAL PREPARATION

Scheduling Trial Testimony of Witnesses

AS SOON AS WE GET a trial date from the court, you should notify our expert witnesses, client, and lay witnesses about the trial date. Our client should be notified by you with a phone call and a letter. If the client has a conflict with the trial date, that's just too bad.

In addition to notifying our clients about the trial date, you should mail a copy of their deposition transcript with a request that they review the transcript as the trial date approaches. The best thing our clients can do to prepare for their trial testimony and cross-examination is to become intimately familiar with their deposition transcript.

You should tell our clients to dress for the trial as if they were going to a funeral—namely, conservative clothing and no jeans, T-shirts, or nose rings. Conservative clothing shows respect and that the trial is very important to our clients.

Scheduling Trial Testimony of Experts

You should call our expert witnesses to get a firm commitment about a date and time for their trial testimony (as soon as we have a trial date from the court). Once you have a date from our expert witnesses, you should confirm the date and time of the expert's trial testimony with a letter.

When you schedule dates for the expert witnesses' trial testimony, you must remind the experts with a letter to bring their entire file to court when they testify. If the expert witnesses do not bring their entire file to court, they will be precluded from giving testimony.

Why it's done this way: If you do not confirm the date of the experts' trial testimony, the experts will try to back out of their trial testimony by claiming that you never confirmed a date with them. A letter to the experts is the best way to confirm that a firm date was selected and approved by the experts.

If experts require a retainer check before they will confirm a date for their trial testimony, you should send me an e-mail, and I will respond to the request with an e-mail to you. You should ask the experts to specify whether the retainer check is nonrefundable— namely, if the case settles, the expert still keeps the entire retainer funds.

Our liability experts should be scheduled to testify on the third or fourth day of the first week of the trial. Jury selection usually takes the entire first day of the trial and opening statements consume the morning of the second day of the trial. The safest bet is to schedule the liability experts beginning with the third day of the trial.

You should not schedule more than one expert witness per day. If you schedule more than one expert to testify at the trial on a single day, I may not have enough time to get both experts' testimony.

You should schedule the trial testimony of damages experts— namely, treating physicians, economist, life care planner—immediately following the testimony of the liability experts.

When you schedule a date for our expert's trial testimony, you must make sure our experts have a complete set of the deposition transcripts and medical records. You should send an e-mail or fax to the experts listing every deposition transcript and medical record in our client's case and ask the experts to confirm that they have all of the records listed in your letter.

Why it's done this way: There is nothing worse than meeting with experts the evening before their trial testimony and learning that they never received four crucial deposition transcripts from me, or they were never sent parts of our client's medical records. I don't need those headaches. It is your job to make sure our experts have all of the records—namely, deposition transcripts and medical records.

Organization of Records for Trial

At least one week before trial, you should put all of the medical records in a large binder with the medical providers (doctors and hospitals) separately tabbed and indexed for identification.

At least one week before trial, you should put all deposition transcripts in a large binder with each deposition transcript separately tabbed and indexed for identification.

At least one week before trial, you should put all pleadings (i.e., summons and complaint, answers, and bills of particulars), discovery responses, and expert responses for all parties in a large binder with each document separately tabbed and indexed for identification.

Why it's done this way: While we are a paperless office, I like having three binders with hard copies of the most important records handy at all times. What can I say? Some habits die hard.

Supplemental Bill of Particulars

You should prepare a supplemental bill of particulars at least 45 days before the first day of the trial. The supplemental bill of particulars will list all of the new medical providers and dates of treatment since our client's last bill of particulars. You should identify the new medical providers and dates of treatment by bolding them in the supplemental bill of particulars, which will make it easy for me to identify the new information that has been added.

My deadline to serve the supplemental bill of particulars is 30 days before the first day of the trial. If we miss this deadline, I will not be permitted to introduce any evidence or testimony concerning our client's new medical treatment. This is legal malpractice!

I will not review the supplemental bill of particulars. I expect you to have all of the new medical providers and dates of treatment in the supplemental bill of particulars, and the only thing I need to do is sign it.

Marked Pleadings

You should prepare a set of marked pleadings, as required by the Uniform Rules of Trial Courts, so I can hand deliver the marked pleadings to the judge on the first day of the trial. Preferably, you will mail the marked pleadings to the judge during the week before the trial date.

Why it's done this way: We want to show the judge and opposing counsel that we are prepared and we know what we are doing. Getting the marked pleadings to the judge during the week before the trial is a good sign that we are ready and prepared for trial.

Jury Verdict Sheet, Proposed Jury Charge, and the Plaintiff's Statement of Contentions

You should prepare a draft of the jury verdict sheet and the proposed jury charge for my review at least five days before the first day of the trial. I have forms for the verdict sheet and proposed jury charge for every kind of case. I will prepare the plaintiff's statement of contentions, since it varies greatly from case to case.

I want to provide the verdict sheet, jury charge, and the plaintiff's statement of contentions no later than the Friday before the first day of the trial.

Records Subpoenaed for Trial

When you subpoena records for a trial, the subpoena should be returnable at least one week before the trial date. This will give me time to review the subpoenaed records and their certifications before the trial.

You should prepare a list of all records that you have subpoenaed for the trial, and you should attach the affidavits of service to the list of subpoenaed records. I will need the list of subpoenaed records and the affidavits of service when I view the subpoenaed records at the Supreme Court clerk's office before the trial.

Scheduling Lay Witnesses for Trial Testimony

Three weeks before the trial date, you should prepare a list of witnesses with the date that each witness will testify.

You should not schedule any witnesses to testify on the first day of the trial. The first day of the trial is reserved for jury selection.

The first witness should be scheduled for the second day of the trial at 1:00 p.m. Opening statements are usually given during the morning of the second day of the trial.

You should send directions to the courthouse to the witnesses and ask them to dress conservatively (as if attending a funeral). You should tell the witnesses to ask the security personnel at the entrance of the courthouse where the courtroom is located, and I will meet them in the courtroom.

Travel for Expert Witnesses

You should always call expert witnesses to ask if they want you to schedule their travel for the trial. Many experts prefer to make their own travel arrangements, but just as often, they will ask you to do this.

If the expert witness wants you to make the travel arrangements, you should purchase and confirm all of the travel of the expert, including a car service to the airport, a plane ticket, hotel reservation, and car service to and from the courthouse.

You should always have the expert witnesses arrive at the airport closest to the courthouse and arrange to have them meet with me the night *before* their trial testimony. I never want the experts to arrive for their trial testimony on the morning of their testimony. That does not give me enough time to meet with them.

Why it's done this way: You always want to stay on the good side of our experts. Enough said.

Scheduling Focus Groups

When I ask you to schedule a focus group for an upcoming trial, I will give you the name of a contact person at a local community organization, for example, a high school or fire department.

I will need at least 15–20 people to attend a focus group. Ideally, the focus group participants are unrelated (i.e., no spouses) and represent a broad cross-section of the community ranging in age from early twenties to seventies with a roughly equal mix of males and females (just like a real jury).

You should always assume that at least twenty percent who have made a commitment to attend the focus group will be no-shows. If you have commitments from 15 persons to attend a focus group, it's a safe bet that only 10–11 will show up.

You should order four pizzas with one plain, one vegetarian, and two meat pizzas, and four two-liter bottles of soda (diet and regular), and plastic plates, cups, and utensils.

9

SETTLEMENTS

Requesting Final Bills from Experts

WHEN A CASE SETTLES, you must fax a letter to all of our expert witnesses with a request that they *stop working on the case* and fax their final invoice to us within 48 hours. You should explain in your letter that the expert witnesses should call us if they are not able to send their final invoice via fax within 48 hours.

It is your job to get the final invoices from all of our experts and vendors in order to ensure we get reimbursed for those expenses at the end of the case.

Confirming the Settlement

It has always been my policy to settle cases either on the record or with a written agreement signed on behalf of the plaintiffs and defendants that expressly states that the written agreement contains all of the terms and conditions of the settlement. Any other "settlement" is not binding on anyone.

You should always make sure that you possess a letter signed by the defense counsel confirming the settlement. If the settlement was placed on the record in open court, you should request a copy of the transcript by calling the court reporter and having the transcript e-mailed to us.

Whether the stipulation of settlement is signed by defense counsel or placed on the record in open court, the terms of the settlement should state as follows:

It is hereby stipulated and agreed, by and on behalf of the plaintiffs and the defendants in this action, [name of defendants] in consideration of the settlement of this action by the plaintiffs and the defendants [name of settling defendants], as follows:

1. The settlement agreement shall have the same effect as if entered into in open court;

2. The attorneys for the respective parties have actual authority to enter into this stipulation of settlement on behalf of their respective clients;

3. The plaintiffs agree to settle their claims against defendants, [name of settling defendants], upon payment on or behalf of this defendant in the sum of [settlement amount] Dollars;

4. Plaintiffs and defendants, [name of settling defendants], hereby agree and acknowledge that this is a settlement of all of the plaintiffs' disputed claims; that no portion of this settlement is allocated for, nor does it include, reimbursement for medical expenses or loss of earnings; that such settlement does not

constitute an admission of fault on the part of defendants, [name of settling defendants];

5. Plaintiffs will defend, indemnify and hold harmless defendants, [name of settling defendants], and their insurance carrier and attorneys, against any enforceable lien, claim or action arising from the settlement or asserted against the settlement proceeds. Plaintiffs shall have the sole responsibility to satisfy any enforceable lien or claim asserted against the settlement proceeds or arising from the settlement;

6. No terms, language or agreement herein shall be construed or interpreted as an acknowledgment that any enforceable lien, claim or action arising from the settlement or asserted against the settlement exists at law or in equity.

Why it's done this way: If I do not have a letter signed by the defense counsel confirming the settlement, or the settlement is not placed on the record in open court, there is no settlement. *Verbal settlements with an insurance adjuster or defense counsel are unenforceable.* There is no enforceable settlement until all of the terms of the settlement are confirmed in writing.

If the defense counsel has not signed a letter confirming the settlement, you should e-mail or fax the stipulation of settlement to defense counsel and ask that it be signed and returned by fax to you.

What to Do When a Case Settles

As soon as the case settles, you should prepare a general release and a stipulation of discontinuance. You should have our client sign the general release *on the same day* that the case settles (unless the case involves an infant settlement or wrongful death for which court approval of the settlement is required).

You should never mail the release agreement to our client. Ideally, you should ask our client to come to our office to sign the release agreement. But if our client has no transportation or resides more than one hour away, you should make arrangements to have the release agreement hand-delivered to our client for signing before a notary public (this might be you).

Once the release agreement is signed by our client before a notary public and I sign the stipulation of discontinuance, you should send the *originals* of the release agreement and stipulation of discontinuance to defense counsel *by certified mail, return receipt requested.* In cases involving an infant settlement or wrongful death, you must also mail the court order approving the settlement with the general release and stipulation of discontinuance.

Tracking the Defendant's Deadline to Send the Settlement Check

When you receive the green receipt card from the U.S. Postal Office, you should calculate the defendants' deadline to mail the settlement check—21 days from their receipt of the general release and stipulation of discontinuance. (In wrongful death and infant settlement cases, you must enclose the court order approving the settlement with the general release and stipulation of discontinuance). Defense counsel has twenty-one days from receipt of the general release and stipulation of discontinuance to mail the settlement check to me.

As the defendant's deadline to mail the settlement check approaches within 2–3 days, you should send a letter via facsimile, reminding the defense counsel that the deadline to mail the settlement check is about to expire and that our client reserves the right to enter judgment against the settling defendant if the deadline is not met.

Settlement Checklist

Before the client is given the settlement check, you must complete a settlement checklist. The settlement check list is checked to ensure that there are no outstanding disbursements.

After you review the settlement checklist, you should sign the checklist at the bottom and give the checklist to the assigned lawyer. The settlement checklist will be reviewed and signed by the lawyer and given to our payroll clerk, before the settlement check can be issued to the client.

Why it's done this way: If you do not make sure all disbursements have been paid before the settlement checks are issued to our client, we will not be reimbursed for disbursements. That's never a good thing, since we are not a charity.

Settlement Statement

You should also prepare a settlement statement that itemizes the gross settlement, disbursements, legal fee, lien amount (i.e., money to be held in our escrow account for the lien) and our client's net recovery. You should annex an itemized list of the disbursements to the settlement statement; you can print the itemization of disbursements under the Costs tab in Trialworks. You should e-mail the settlement statement to me for my review and approval before it is signed by our client.

The settlement statement must be signed by the client and me before the settlement check can be hand-delivered to our client. You should give a copy of the settlement statement to our client.

Clients Must Sign a "Grillo" Waiver

Before the settlement checks are given to our clients, you must prepare a Grillo waiver. A Grillo waiver is a document that should be signed by the clients wherein they acknowledge they have been informed about the benefits of a structured settlement annuity and they have opted against the annuity.

The "Grillo" waiver states:

1. I acknowledge that I have been given an opportunity to meet with a financial consultant of my choice.

2. I am aware that the law enables all principal and interest earned in a structured settlement annuity to be excluded from my gross income and that this opportunity is only available to persons like me who are recovering tort damages on account of a physical injury or physical sickness that I or an immediate family member have suffered.

3. I understand that, if I do not participate in a structured settlement, all earnings on any investment that I may choose could be fully taxed at my highest income tax bracket.

4. My attorney has warned me of the pitfalls of not selecting a portion of my recovery to be included in a structured settlement annuity and has informed me that due to unexpected events or circumstances, many plaintiffs who do not participate in a structured settlement annuity either lose their money award due to investment risks and/or deplete their funds and lose financial security.

5. I understand that this is my only opportunity to take advantage of a structured settlement annuity and that my settlement decision cannot be changed or reversed on a future date in that it is irrevocable. I have been given every opportunity to ask questions and all my questions have been answered.

6. I acknowledge and understand that after being fully informed of my options that by signing my name, I agree to either [ ] reject the structured settlement annuity option and accept a one-time lump sum payment option; or [ ] wish to evaluate structure settlement annuity option/evaluate quotes.

Why it's done this way: If I fail to inform our clients about the option of investing some or all of their settlement money in a structured settlement annuity, I will be sued for legal malpractice. Ninety-eight percent of our clients will lose all of their settlement money within two years and when that happens, they will be looking for someone to blame (that's us!). In order to avoid a legal malpractice claim, you must make sure our clients sign the Grillo waiver before they get their settlement check.

NEVER agree to Confidentiality:

We NEVER agree to confidentiality in any settlement. In 21 years of practice, I have never agreed to confidentiality in a single case nor will this ever happen. This is non-negotiable in every case.

There are TWO BIG REASONS we never agree to confidentiality:

- Secret settlements allow bad doctors to hide their malpractice from the public;

- Secret settlements expose injury victims to income tax liability on their settlements.

The fundamental purpose of injury litigation is thwarted by secret and confidential settlements. A bad doctor can hide one malpractice settlement after the next with confidential settlements and the public will have no information about the doctor's malpractice history. A bad doctor can have a string of malpractice settlements but if the settlements are confidential, the public has no way of knowing.

It is not enough to get a good result for our client—the goal of malpractice litigation is to improve the quality of medical care for all patients. Confidential settlements do nothing to establish a standard of care for future cases or help improve medical care for others. For this reason alone, I will never agree to confidentiality.

As if that's not enough: all consideration for confidentiality is taxable income to our client. Amos v. Commissioner, Tax Court Memo. LEXIS 330 (2003). Although payment to settle a personal injury case is not taxable under the Internal Revenue Code, compensation paid for confidentiality is taxable income to our clients. Even if you agree to partial confidentiality (limited to the amount of the settlement), the injury victim is still subject to some income tax liability.

26 U.S.C.A. section 104(a)(2) provides that gross income does not include "the amount of any damages (other than punitive damages)...on account of personal physical injuries or physical sickness." Pursuant to 26 U.S.C.A. section 104(a)(2), our clients have the right to expect that their personal injury settlements will not be subject to income taxes. But if a portion of a settlement is allocated to confidentiality, our clients will have to pay income taxes on at least a part of their settlement...and we will be faced with a legal malpractice lawsuit.

The simple way to avoid these headaches? Never agree to confidentiality at any costs.

However, when a case settles, we will agree to the following conditions provided our clients give their consent:

It is stipulated and agreed that none of the parties have requested, nor have they agreed to, confidentiality as part of the consideration for the settlement of this matter.

The parties and their attorneys do voluntarily represent to each other and to the court that:

▫ They will not affirmatively seek to disseminate information regarding this settlement or its terms to the news media;

▫ For purposes of this representation, the term "news media" is used to describe print media (newspapers, magazines), broadcast media (radio station, television stations, television networks), but shall not refer to any news media whose primary attention is the members of the legal profession or the insurance industry, or the website, www.protectingpatientrights, and print newsletter, Lawyer Alert, of the law firm of John H. Fisher, P.C.;

▫ It is expressly understood and agreed that this voluntary representation is not a condition of, and does not form any part of the consideration for, the settlement of this matter;

▫ It is also expressly and understood that this voluntary representation shall not be enforceable by action or proceeding, whether in law or equity, in any state or federal court;

▫ This voluntary representation constitutes the complete agreement and understanding between the parties regarding the settlement and the parties have not entered into any other agreements, understandings or representations.

NEVER use defense brokers in structured settlements

We recommend against settling any case that involves the purchase of an annuity through the use of a broker who does not represent the interests of the plaintiff. The reason for this policy is that the broker "owes no duty" to the plaintiff. The broker's only duty is to the defendant, or more precisely, to the defendants' insurance company.

There are occasions when it makes sense to use an annuity as part of a settlement. However, such an annuity should not be recommended unless the plaintiff is free to select the broker, is free to negotiate the fee with the broker (the customary fee on an annuity is 4%—however, when the broker does not have to split the fee with a defense broker there is usually room to negotiate a better fee on behalf of the plaintiff); and usually, when the plaintiff's broker is able to get the plaintiff "rated" at a much higher age.

If the plaintiff can be "rated" for a structured settlement annuity, it must be by a plaintiff's only broker. The reason is that the defense broker has no obligation to disclose what the "real" rating is. This is another way that the defense brokers are able to save money for their clients.

Do NOT include insurance companies on the release agreement

Unless specifically bargained for, you should not include the defendant's insurance company on the release agreement.

Why it's done this way: The defendant's insurance company is not a defendant in the lawsuit and the plaintiff has no claims against it. Hence, it is completely pointless to name the defendant's insurance company as one of the settling parties on the release agreement or stipulation of settlement.

10

HOW TO KEEP CLIENTS HAPPY: THE FIVE-STEP CLIENT CARE SYSTEM

"The first rule of any technology used in a business is that automation applied to an efficient operation will magnify the efficiency."

—BILL GATES

Why You Need an Automated System for Following Up with Clients

INSTEAD OF JUST GIVING YOU a little taste of our follow-up campaign (before and after the filing of the lawsuit), you're going to get, verbatim, the content that I created to keep clients informed of the status of their case. The five-step follow-up campaign sends updates explaining the important milestones of the case. But we're not just talking e-mail updates. The clients get direct mail, a book, and audio CDs with valuable content about the procedures of a lawsuit.

Why do we do this? Simple: because no other lawyer does. And keep in mind one important point: if you automate the process of educating your clients, you won't be bothered with the endless phone calls and e-mails asking you what a deposition is, or what your client should wear to his deposition. The automated education process makes you look good to your clients and frees up more time for you to spend with your family.

Follow-Up Campaign *before* the Lawsuit

FIRST E-MAIL TO PROSPECTIVE CLIENT *BEFORE* THE LAWSUIT IS FILED: INITIAL THANK-YOU E-MAIL FOR A NEW CLIENT

Thank you for the opportunity to evaluate your case.

I am extremely selective and I decline roughly 98 percent of all new cases, so I am excited to take the next step with you of getting your medical records in order to evaluate your potential case.

The first step will be to get the medical records. This can take some time, but we have an excellent team that will be request-ing the medical records and following up with the doctors and hospitals to avoid any delays.

If you would like to speak with me, I will always make myself available to you but only when you follow my specific rules for communication, known as "The Three Rules of Communication," a copy of which is attached to this e-mail. This is an important document, so I ask that you read "The Three Rules of Commu-nication" carefully. If you'd like a hard copy of my rules for com-munication, just send an e-mail to my paralegal at cskidmore@ fishermalpracticelaw.com and we will be happy to send you as many hard copies as you want.

As our special thank-you for this opportunity, we are attaching to this e-mail the document, "Your Eight Basic Rights," which gives you the inside information about your rights in a personal injury and medical malpractice case. If you'd like a hard copy of "Your Eight Basic Rights," just send an e-mail to us and we will be happy to mail as many hard copies as you want.

If you ever have any questions, complaints or concerns, please let me know and I will do my best to address them.

Thank you again for this opportunity.

SECOND E-MAIL TO PROSPECTIVE CLIENT *BEFORE* THE LAWSUIT IS FILED: MAILING OF RELEASE AUTHORIZATIONS TO GET MEDICAL RECORDS.

Today, we requested your medical records.

It usually takes two to three weeks to get the medical records (although New York's Public Health Law requires the production of the records within ten days, we would be shocked if that happened). My best estimate is that it will take at least two weeks to get your medical records from your doctor or hospital.

No need to worry. If we don't get your medical records within the time permitted by New York law, our team will send some friendly reminder letters to the doctor or hospital within ten days of the initial request and some not-so-friendly phone-call and letter warnings after the deadline passes. If we suspect that the doctor or hospital has not provided us with all of your records, our team may do an "original chart review" to inspect your original medical records at the doctor's office.

What happens to your medical records once we get them? Your privacy and confidentiality rights will be carefully protected under the "Rules for Protecting your Privacy and Confidentiality Rights," a copy of which is attached to this e-mail.

When we receive the medical records, your medical records will be scanned into our computer system, and you can request a paper copy or electronic copy of your medical records whenever and as often as you want. We are here to serve you, so please don't hesitate to ask if you would like a copy of your medical records.

Our team will be on contact with you as soon as we receive your medical records. In the meantime, if you have any questions or just want a status report, you can always feel free to call or e-mail my paralegal.

Just thought you'd like to know.

THIRD E-MAIL TO PROSPECTIVE CLIENT *BEFORE* THE LAWSUIT IS FILED: RECEIPT OF MEDICAL RECORDS.

At last! Today, we received the remaining medical records from your medical providers.

Your medical records have been scanned into our computer system, and you can have a paper or electronic copy of your records whenever you want. Remember, the "Rules for Protecting Your Privacy and Confidentiality Rights" explains how we handle your medical records and protect your confidentiality and privacy rights.

We now have a complete set of your medical records, which we need to evaluate your case. Here's what happens next:

- My paralegal will review your medical records to confirm that your doctor or hospital provided all of the medical records that we requested. (We often get an incomplete set of medical records and have to make second and third requests for your medical records.) This will take place within one to two days after we receive your medical records.

- I will review your medical records to confirm that the information that you provided to us about your case is consistent with the medical records. For example, occasionally, a new client's history of symptoms and complaints—for example, chest pain—is not documented in the medical records. When the symptoms and complaints are not documented in your medical records, it is very difficult to prove that your doctor violated the standard of care.

▫ In most cases, I will provide a copy of your medical records to my medical expert (a surgeon with tremendous insights in medical legal cases and it never hurts to have two sets of eyes reviewing your case, right?).

▫ After I complete the review of your potential case, I will contact you to discuss our evaluation of your case—namely, whether your doctor deviated from the standard of care and if so, whether the deviation from the standard of care caused injury to you. This is just lawyer-talk for, "Did your doctor violate the rules and if so, were you hurt?"

The review of your case may take a little time, so we will appreciate your patience. Some cases are more complicated than others, so you may not get an immediate answer about your case. If that happens, just call or e-mail my paralegal to schedule a time to speak with me.

Just keep in mind, you may have insights into your case that may be missed by the highest paid and best doctors in the world. If you suspect that my team and I have missed something in our case review, just let me know. You may be right.

FOURTH E-MAIL TO PROSPECTIVE CLIENT *BEFORE* THE LAWSUIT IS FILED: READY TO DISCUSS OUR REVIEW OF THE CASE.

We are ready to discuss your case with you!

We have completed our review your medical records and I am ready to discuss your case with you. Let's schedule a time to talk.

Just to make sure we make the most productive use of our time, please send me via fax (845-802-0052) or e-mail (jfisher@fishermalpracticelaw.com) the specific questions that you want me to address, and I will make sure all of your questions have been answered during our meeting or phone appointment. If you don't have any specific questions, that's no problem.

If you have a family member you would like to have listen to our conversation, that's fine. Just send an e-mail to my paralegal to let her know first, and I will be happy to accommodate your request.

Please call my paralegal at 845-802-0047, and she will schedule a time for us to meet or speak by phone.

I look forward to speaking with you.

FIFTH E-MAIL TO PROSPECTIVE CLIENT *BEFORE* THE LAWSUIT IS FILED: ACCEPTANCE OF NEW CASE

Congratulations! We have accepted your case and we are preparing to file your lawsuit.

In my first e-mail to you, I attached documents titled "The Three Rules of Communication" and "Your Eight Basic Rights." Now that I have accepted your case, we need to formalize our relationship by signing these documents. In a few days, you will receive a letter from me with enclosures of "The Three Rules of Communication" and "Your Eight Basic Rights."

When you receive this letter from us, I ask that you sign "The Three Rules of Communication" where indicated and return the original to me in the enclosed, self-addressed, stamped envelope. When I receive the fully signed "Three Rules of Communication" from you, you will be mailed a copy of the agreement. Please keep the copy handy and make sure you are intimately familiar with my rules for communication. *This may be the most important document you will sign.*

In the mail, you will also receive the document known as "Your Eight Basic Rights" that provides you with all of your rights in our attorney-client relationship. This is my special gift to you, and as my way of showing my commitment to these rules, I signed or initialed every page of "Your Eight Basic Rights."

If you ever have any question whether I am providing you with *all* of the rights listed in "Your Eight Basic Rights," I want you to make sure I am aware of it. Remember, I will always be willing to address your concerns or questions, but only if you make me aware of them.

Just to make sure you still have it, you will also receive in the mail the document known as the "Rules for Protecting Your Privacy and Confidentiality Rights," which explains how your privacy and confidentiality rights will be protected by our team. I hope you enjoy it.

I look forward to moving your lawsuit forward with your help.

Why it's done this way: We always want to *dazzle* our clients and give them a "Wow!" experience with us. The five-step client care system provides a system for keeping clients informed about the status of our case review with minimal effort on your end. All of the work is done by Infusionsoft and our fulfillment provider, Help Without Hassle. It's that simple.

Follow Up Campaign *after* the Lawsuit Is Filed

The five-step client care system *after the filing of the lawsuit* ensures that our clients are aware of the status of their case at each important milestone of their lawsuit.

FIRST E-MAIL TO CLIENT *AFTER* THE LAWSUIT IS FILED:

Congratulations! Your lawsuit was filed today.

The summons and complaint will be served upon the defendants and the defendants will have 30 days to respond to the complaint with a legal document known as an answer. The answer is that response to the allegations contained in the complaint.

You will hear from us as soon as we have the answers of the defendants. In the meantime, please don't hesitate to call my paralegal at 845-802-0047, if you have any questions.

By the way, there is no need to worry if we don't have answers from the defendants within 30 days, since it is not unusual for the defendants to request an extension of their deadline to respond to your complaint.

As a special thanks, in a few days you will receive in the mail my book, *The Seven Deadly Mistakes of Malpractice Victims*, and my audio CD, "How to Win Your Lawsuit against a Doctor," which I know you will enjoy.

My book and audio CD give you the insider tips and secrets about the most common mistakes made by medical malpractice and injury victims and how you can avoid these mistakes from happening in your case. If you would like extra copies of my book or audio CD, just send an e-mail to my paralegal at cskidmore@fishermalpracticelaw.com or call Corina at 845-802-0047, and she will be happy to send you as many books and CDs that you want.

SECOND E-MAIL TO CLIENT *AFTER* THE LAWSUIT IS FILED: RECEIPT OF THE DEFENDANT'S ANSWERS.

Today, we received the defendant's answer in your lawsuit.

Now, there will be a lot of paperwork exchanged between the lawyers. This is called discovery. As part of discovery, we will serve written demands upon the defense lawyers (called discovery demands) and the defense lawyers will serve written demands upon us seeking information about the injuries, medical treatment, and the allegations of negligence.

The process of exchanging the paperwork takes time, but we are working on it. If you would like copies of the discovery demands or discovery responses, it's no problem. Just send my paralegal an e-mail at cskidmore@fishermalpracticelaw.com and the paperwork will be e-mailed or if it's too voluminous, she will mail a compact disc containing the paperwork.

We will be in contact with you to schedule a date for your deposition as soon as the discovery is complete.

We always like to stay in contact with you so don't forget to call us if you have any had new medical treatment or just want to chat. Remember, we're here to help you, so it's not a bother at all.

THIRD E-MAIL TO CLIENT *AFTER* THE LAWSUIT IS FILED: CONFIRM DATE OF DEPOSITION.

Great news! Today, we scheduled your deposition!

At your deposition, the defense lawyers will get to ask questions about your case. Don't worry. I will be at the deposition to protect your rights and make sure everything goes well.

My paralegal will call or e-mail you to schedule a date and time for us to meet to help you prepare for your deposition. It will be best if we meet about one week before the deposition so you have a good idea what questions will be asked at your deposition and what you can expect. If you prefer to meet at your home, that's usually not a problem. Just ask my paralegal for a meeting at your home and don't be afraid to ask for a specific time. (I can usually accommodate your schedule.)

I will answer all of your questions about the deposition at our meeting. But in the meantime, if you have specific concerns that you want me to answer before our meeting, please call or e-mail my paralegal, and we will be happy to schedule a phone appointment so we can talk.

FOURTH E-MAIL TO CLIENT *AFTER* THE LAWSUIT IS FILED: CONFIRMING THAT WE ARE NOW ASKING FOR A TRIAL DATE.

YES! Discovery is complete and today we filed a request for a trial date with the court.

The court will schedule a court conference in order to schedule a date for your trial. If there are certain dates when you cannot attend the trial—for example, you will be away on vacation— please call my paralegal ASAP and let us know. We can usually accommodate your schedule, but only if you let us know *before* the court conference.

Remember, once the trial date is scheduled by the court, it is "set in stone" and we cannot change it. So if you have any dates when you are simply not available for the trial, please let us know.

When I have a date for your trial, we will be in contact with you about the trial date.

FIFTH E-MAIL TO CLIENT *AFTER* THE LAWSUIT IS FILED: NOTIFYING CLIENT OF THE DATE OF THE TRIAL.

Congratulations!

Today, the court scheduled your trial for May 6.

As the trial date approaches, we will be in contact with you in order to help you prepare for the trial. But relax and try to forget about the trial until we get closer to the trial date.

The best way that you can prepare for the trial is to read and re-read your deposition transcript as often as possible. You want to almost memorize your deposition transcript so that your testimony at the trial does not contradict your deposition testimony. If you need another copy of your deposition transcript, please call or e-mail my paralegal and she will be happy to e-mail or mail your transcript to you.

If you know someone who you believe might make a good witness for your trial, please let us know, and I will make sure we meet with them. We have to notify the defense of any witnesses that we intend to have testify at your trial, so please let us know now if there are witnesses who you believe might be willing to testify at the trial.

Remember, if you have any questions and want to meet, I will always be happy to schedule a meeting or phone appointment with you. Just e-mail or call my paralegal, and we will schedule an appointment for you.

Why it's done this way: Our goal is to *overcommunicate* with clients. We want our clients to be dazzled and blown away by their experience with us, so they will rave about us to their friends and neighbors (resulting in more referrals from their "sphere of influence").

How to Automate Follow-Up for Your Law Practice

Infusionsoft is a software system designed for automated follow-up to your prospective clients with e-mails, direct mail, fax, voice broadcast, and even text messaging. Once you create a follow-up sequence, you can create the follow-up in Infusionsoft. Then, Infusionsoft will send the automated e-mails to your prospective clients and notify your fulfillment provider whenever a piece of direct mail or a postcard needs to be mailed to a new client. (A "fulfillment provider" responds to requests for your free offers by direct mail. I use Help Without Hassle, based in Kansas.)

"Without follow-up systems in place, you don't have stability in your business ... You have chaos."

—**CLATE MASK (CEO OF INFUSIONSOFT)**, *Conquer the Chaos*

Infusionsoft will keep a database of all new clients who contact you, and track the number of e-mails and direct mail, and so on, which have been sent to the prospective client. Now, your law firm is operating on autopilot and e-mails, faxes, text messages, and direct mail are being sent to new clients while you're sleeping. You just mastered the follow-up process with no work other than the initial set up with Infusionsoft.

Part 2
THE MANAGER
(HOW TO MANAGE THE LAW FIRM OF YOUR DREAMS)

*"Mediocrity results first and foremost
from management failure."*

—JIM COLLINS, *Good to Great*

11

THE KEY
PERFORMANCE
INDICATORS FOR
SUCCESS

"Begin by quantifying everything related to how you do business ... You can't ask too many questions about the numbers."

—MICHAEL E. GERBER, *The E-Myth Revisited*

HOW CAN I TELL if we are accomplishing our goals? How do I track your performance?

There are four metrics (key performance indicators) that you should track in every lawsuit, in four categories:

1. discovery responses

2. depositions

3. completion of discovery

4. completion of the trial

1. **Discovery responses**: How many days does it take between (a) our receipt of the defendant's discovery demands, and the (b) service of the plaintiff's discovery responses?

2. **Depositions**: How many days does it take between the (a) service of the plaintiff's discovery responses, and the (b) first deposition?

3. **Completion of discovery**: How many days does it take between our (a) receipt of the defendant's answer, and (b) the filing of the note of issue?

4. **Completion of the Lawsuit**: How many days does it take between (a) the filing of the lawsuit, and (b) the first day of trial (or the settlement of the case if that occurs)?

In every lawsuit, it is your job to document the number of days that it takes for each of the four categories and generate a memo in Trialworks listing the number of days that it took to complete each of the four categories of key performance indicators. For example, if we receive the defendant's discovery responses on September 30 and we serve the plaintiff's discovery responses and bill of particulars on November 7, it took *38 days* for us to serve the plaintiff's discovery responses (category 1: discovery responses).

> *"Every company that employs people can (and should) develop measurable performance criteria."*
>
> —Dan Kennedy, *No B.S. Ruthless Management of People & Profits*

By the end of the lawsuit, you should have documented the number of days that it took to complete each of the four key performance indicators. For example, you should prepare a memorandum that states the number of days that it took for service of the plaintiff's discovery responses and bill of particulars (category 1), the number of days between the service of the plaintiff's discovery responses and the first deposition (category 2), the number of days between our receipt of the defendant's answer and the filing of the note of issue (category 3), and the number of days between the filing of the summons and complaint and the first day of trial (category 4).

Your memo should have the subject line, "The Key Performance Indicators for this Case" and list the number of days that it took for each of the four categories.

Why it's done this way: From the beginning of the case until its end, *everything must be measured!* We do not measure our success just by the end result—namely, the amount of money recovered for the client. *Our success is measured by the number of days that it took to get the result.* A great outcome for the client isn't so great if it took five years to get it.

What Are Our Key Performance Indicators (aka Goals for the Lawsuit)?

Our goal is simple: *get to trial as quickly as possible.* Our clients will not get a result until the trial date (or in some cases just a day or two before the trial date), so it is our *number-one goal* to get the case to trial as quickly as possible.

So, how do we accomplish our goal? Simple: *we must comply with deadlines.*

Am I referring to deadlines imposed by the court in a preliminary conference stipulation and order? No! Those deadlines are too lax and are constantly violated by defense lawyers. If we simply live by the rules of the court and defense counsel, we are playing right into their hands—namely, we can expect long delays and adjournments of the case. This does not work for me!

The deadlines that we must live are created by me. My rules are not unrealistic, but you will not accomplish these goals by sitting back and letting the defense lawyers control the progress of the lawsuit.

There are specific measurable goals for each of the four key performance indicators. The goals for each category are:

1. **Discovery responses**: How many days does it take between (a) our receipt of the defendant's discovery demands, and (b) the service of the plaintiff's discovery responses? **30 DAYS.**

2. **Depositions**: How many days does it take between (a) the service of the plaintiff's discovery responses, and (b) the first deposition? **90 DAYS.**

3. **Completion of discovery**: How many days does it take between (a) our receipt of the defendant's answer, and (b) the filing of the note of issue? **180 DAYS.**

4. **Completion of the lawsuit**: How many days does it take between (a) the filing of the lawsuit, and (b) the first day of trial (or the settlement of the case if that occurs)? **ONE YEAR AND SIX MONTHS.**

At the end of every lawsuit, you will complete a flow chart that lists the number of days that it took to complete each of the four key performance indicators for the case. Now, I know it's not easy and there are certain things outside your control (such as the court's trial calendar), but you are working at an exceptional law firm, and we have exceptional standards and expectations. You should always seek to meet each of the four key performance indicators.

At the end of every lawsuit, you should complete the flow chart listing each of the four key performance indicators and sign and date the flow chart and e-mail the completed flow chart to me. Until I review the flow chart, the case is not over.

One word of caution: we do not control the scheduling of the trial date. In some counties in New York it will not be possible to get a trial date that is within one year of the filing of the note of issue. But in most counties it is realistic that our trial date will be scheduled at least within 12 months from the date that the note of issue was filed.

Why it's done this way: We must have measurable, attainable goals for our cases. Now, you should have no questions about the deadlines for each of the four key performance indicators.

How to Manage a Budget for Every Lawsuit

Every case that we "accept" must have a budget. A case is "accepted" when three things occur: (1) the client signs a retainer agreement, (2) the case is moved from "under consideration" to "in suit" in Trialworks, and (3) we file the summons and complaint. It is not necessary to have a case budget for cases that are "under consideration" in Trialworks—namely, cases we have not decided to accept and for which we have not filed a lawsuit.

Once a case is "accepted," a case budget must be created under the Memorandum tab in Trialworks. The case budget has three phases:

1. discovery phase

2. trial preparation phase

3. trial phase

DISCOVERY PHASE:

The discovery phase includes all expenses between the filing of the summons and complaint and the filing of the note of issue. The discovery phase will include, among other things, estimated expenses for filing fees, stenographer and videographer fees for depositions, expert fees for reviewing the case, and fees of damages experts for a life care plan and an economic report of damages.

TRIAL PREPARATION PHASE:

The trial preparation phase will include all expenses between the filing of the note of issue and the first day of the trial. The typical expenses in the trial preparation phase include expert witness fees, expenses associated with courtroom exhibits, and the medical experts' fees to examine our client before trial.

TRIAL PHASE:

The trial phase includes all expenses incurred between the first day of the trial and the conclusion of the lawsuit. The trial phase typically includes fees for the trial testimony of expert witnesses, the fee of the court reporter for transcripts of trial testimony, and the hotel and travel expenses of our expert witnesses and fact witnesses.

The case budget will be prepared by the paralegal assigned to the case and reviewed by the lawyer. It is important to try to be as precise as possible with the estimated costs. If, for example, you are trying to estimate the fees of neurosurgeons for trial testimony, you should call the neurosurgeons' assistants to ask for estimates of all of their fees, including their time spent reviewing the file for their trial testimony, and hotel and travel expenses, and the time they spend at the trial. If the experts have a standard form listing their fees, you should ask the experts to e-mail or fax the form to you, and you can then use the experts' forms for your estimates of the expenses.

Why it's done this way: Before accepting a case, I need to decide whether the new case will provide a good return on investment (ROI). The ROI can only be determined by comparing the anticipated legal fee to the estimated case expenses and the ideal ratio between the legal fee and the case expenses is 10 to 1. I cannot determine the ratio between the anticipated legal fee and the case expenses without a case budget.

How You Should Keep Experts' Fees within Our Budget

Some experts will take advantage of our cases by sending crazy bills with huge fees. I don't have an unlimited budget. The best way to keep a lid on expert fees is the original retainer letter to the expert.

In your original letter to experts, you should state that experts should call or e-mail us before exceeding the retainer check issued to them—namely, "If your review of the medical records will result in a fee that exceeds the retainer check, please call or e-mail John to get his permission before proceeding further with your review."

Why it's done this way: Experts will often milk a file if we give them carte blanche to spend all their time reviewing the case.

12

GETTING THE BEST RESULTS FROM YOUR STAFF

(PERFORMANCE-BASED BONUS COMPENSATION)

"The best results seem to come from very targeted, behavior-based, individual bonus plans."

—DAN KENNEDY, *No B.S. Ruthless Management of People & Profits*

I HAVE A PERFORMANCE-BASED program for incentives and bonuses for each member of my team who is assigned to a case.

The performance-based system for bonus compensation is based upon three crucial factors:

1. timing

2. cost-effectiveness

3. result

All three of these factors must be satisfied in order to qualify for a bonus in an individual case.

TIMING:

The four key performance indicators relate to the speed within which you can complete various phases of a lawsuit. For example, the third key performance indicator, completion of discovery, specifies a deadline of 180 days from the receipt of the defendant's answer until the filing of the note of issue. If, for example, you file the note of issue no more than 180 days after our receipt of the defendant's answer, you've satisfied the third key performance indicator.

Of the four key performance indicators, the most important is the deadline of one year and six months for the completion of the lawsuit from the filing of the lawsuit until the first day of the trial or settlement. *The one-year-and-six-month deadline for the completion of the lawsuit is the gold standard by which your performance will be measured.* When a lawsuit is completed from the filing of the lawsuit until the first day of trial, or settlement within one year and six months, you have satisfied the most important key performance indicator.

In order to qualify for bonus compensation, the lawsuit must be completed within one year and six months from the filing of the lawsuit until the first day of trial. There will always be factors outside your control, such as the court's congested trial calendar or adjournments of trial dates and depositions by the defense lawyers, and that's why this is the most difficult of the three performance-based factors for bonus compensation.

Why it's done this way: Every lawsuit is a "race against time." The defendant's lawyers will stonewall and delay you at every opportunity, but our job is to get the lawsuit to trial as quickly as possible. One year and six months is not an easy deadline to meet for the completion of the lawsuit and you will face obstacles at every juncture of the lawsuit. But if you get the case to trial within one year and six months from the filing of the lawsuit, you have met the first of the three performance-based factors for bonus compensation.

COST-EFFECTIVENESS:

Every case must be managed within a predetermined case budget. The case budget is based upon anticipated case expenses during discovery and trial. At the end of every lawsuit, you must compare our legal fee to the disbursements—namely, case expenses—to determine whether the result meets the criteria for performance-based bonus compensation for an individual lawsuit.

Our goal is to resolve the case with a legal fee to our firm that exceeds the disbursements by a ratio of 10 to 1. If, for example, our legal fee (after payment of referral fees) is $150,000 and the disbursements are $15,000, the ratio of the legal fee to the disbursements is 10 to 1. This is a successful outcome and meets the second of the performance-based factors for bonus compensation.

If, on the other hand, our legal fee is $150,000 and the disbursements are $25,000, the ratio of the legal fee to the disbursements is 6 to 1 and that does not meet our second factor for performance-based bonus compensation.

Why it's done this way: Our goal is to be smart with our clients' money. When we spend money on a lawsuit, we are really spending our clients' money, so we need to be careful and keep expert witnesses within a strict budget. Your performance will be based in part upon whether we keep each case within a budget and meet our goal of our legal fee that exceeds the disbursements by a ratio of 10 to 1.

RESULT:

The most important of the performance-based factors for bonus compensation is the *result*. The *result* is the amount of money that we recover, whether by settlement or judgment, for our client.

At the beginning of every lawsuit, there will be two numbers assigned to each case: 1—the *settlement goal* and 2—the *settlement value* and a number for the settlement goal and the settlement value will be entered under the Case Value tab in Trialworks, so you will always be able to tell what those numbers are.

The *settlement value* is the "rock bottom" final number that sets the floor for settlement negotiations. The lawsuit will not be settled for less than the settlement value unless there is some unforeseen development in the case, for example, the death of our client.

The *settlement goal* is just what the words say: this is the goal for the case. The settlement goal reflects the highest, realistic value for the settlement, and it is always higher than the settlement value.

In order to qualify for bonus compensation, the amount of the recovery, whether by settlement or judgment, *must equal or exceed the settlement goal.* Let's say, for example, that the settlement goal for a case is $1,500,000 and the settlement value is $1,250,000. If the case settles for $1,750,000, you exceeded the settlement goal by $250,000, and you've satisfied the third criteria for performance-based bonus compensation.

Why it's done this way: Even if you meet the first and second of the performance-based factors for bonus compensation, it will not necessarily mean a successful outcome for our client unless the *result* meets our pre-established goals. Ultimately, the most important factor for success is the net amount of money that we recover for our clients and hence, the result is the most important of the three performance-based criteria for bonus compensation.

Reporting the Results at the End of the Lawsuit

At the end of the case, you need to track the results.

When the lawsuit is over, you should prepare a memorandum in Trialworks showing the results in the three categories of timing, cost-effectiveness, and results. Your memorandum should state, for example:

- **Timing**: From the filing of the lawsuit until the settlement or judgment, how long did it take? (Remember, our goal is one year and six months.)

- **Cost-Effectiveness**: What is the ratio between the amount of our legal fee and the disbursements? (The ideal ratio is 10 to 1.)

- **Results**: Did the settlement (or judgment) exceed the *settlement goal* for the case?

So, how did we do? If we meet the three categories for performance-based bonus compensation, you will receive bonus compensation based upon the terms set forth in your *position contract*.

Why it's done this way: You should be rewarded for great performance! The three factors for the performance-based bonus compensation are not easy to meet, but they are attainable.

13

HOW TO MAKE YOUR EMPLOYEES ACCOUNTABLE

"Most employees, regardless of level of responsibility, do much better work when they understand what's expected and have a clear understanding of the routine work."

—John Jantsch, *The Referral Engine*

NEW LEGAL SECRETARIES have a rosy picture of a great new future for their law firm. Your new secretary (we'll call her "Jane") is all smiles and bubbles with enthusiasm. Finally, you're convinced you've found the superstar secretary who will turn everything around for your law practice.

But as time passes, a different picture begins emerging. Your "superstar" employee, Jane, starts showing up to work a few minutes later, and as time passes, she begins leaving just five minutes early. Jane leaves for lunch before her lunch break begins (yes, this always happens), she begins browsing on the Internet to look for places to visit for her next family vacation. Before long, Jane is spending 20 minutes paying her family bills at work.

Things go from bad to worse. You show up at a deposition and Jane has forgotten to call a stenographer or videographer to attend the deposition. Jane's priorities are not your priorities. Before long, you begin wondering what Jane does at work.

> ### *"People will do only one thing predictably—be unpredictable."*
> —MICHAEL E. GERBER, *The E-Myth Revisited*

It's inevitable that Jane's story will not have a happy ending. You begin missing court-ordered deadlines for the completion of depositions, and when you finally confront Jane to ask why the depositions have not been scheduled, she looks puzzled and replies, "I thought you were going to schedule the depositions."

You can't believe your ears. You've had enough and Jane is fired. I know it's easy to just rationalize the bad hire with thoughts such as, "You can't find good help around my town," but who's really to blame for this fiasco?

Why You Must Have a Position Contract for Every Member of Your Staff

If your secretaries, paralegals, and attorneys (and yes, even the janitor) don't have clearly defined rules that explain what is expected of them, they will determine for themselves what to do ... and that's not a good thing.

A position contract explains the specific duties of each of your employees. Let's say you're about to hire a new receptionist. Before she begins work, ask yourself what you expect the new receptionist to do. Now write everything on a piece of paper. In just minutes you've created a position contract.

The position contract for your new receptionist explains with crystal clarity the specific job responsibilities and goes from general (answer phones, schedule depositions) to specific (arrive no later than 9 a.m. and do not leave before 5 p.m.) Try to be as specific as possible when writing the position contract. If you leave any job responsibility to the discretion or judgment of the new receptionist, you can bet that the job won't get done in the way you want it. So, don't leave anything to the judgment or discretion of your new hire.

The Goal of the Position Contract

It's easy to say you don't have time to create a position contract for your new employee. If you don't, it's just a matter of time before your new "superstar" employee doesn't do the work the way you wanted and tells you, "I didn't know you wanted me to do that."

But the biggest mistake you can make is to blame your new employee, even though you can't understand how anyone could possibly think like your new hire. But it's not her fault. You hired her and you never clearly defined, in writing, her job responsibilities.

"A lot of employees who would perform don't, largely because nobody has ever defined what they're supposed to be doing."

—DAN KENNEDY, *No B.S. Ruthless Management of People & Profits*

By creating a clear set of rules for the new hire, you are leaving nothing to chance. There's no possibility that she will come back to you and say, "I didn't know I was supposed to do that." Of course, she did. It's right there in the position contract.

I know what you're thinking. You want to take the easy way out so you think that you'll just have your trusty office manager or paralegal explain the rules of your office to the new employee. Big mistake! Remember, if you don't have a position contract for your other employees, they will teach your new hire all of the things that they are doing (and I'm guessing that might be scary for you). Yes, the new hire will be taught all of the things that your staff thinks the new employee should do, not what you want your new hire to do.

So, do this one thing: write the specific duties and tasks of new employees on a piece of paper so there will not be any doubt as to what is expected of them.

Have New Employees Sign the Position Contract

But just having the position contract is not enough. You have to send two originals of the position contract to all new staff members before they begin the job and ask them to review the position contract. You should ask new hires to sign both originals, return one to you and to keep one original at her desk, preferably posted prominently in front of their desk. These are the rules that they agree to live by, and yes, these are *your rules*.

Your new hires now have a clearly defined set of tasks and duties that leave no room for discretion or judgment. But is this a guarantee that the work will get done the way you want? Well, of course not. But you have now reached a firm understanding with your new hires. If there is any doubt as to what they are expected to do, all they have to do is look at the position contract for answers.

You should have a position contract for every member of your firm. From the custodial maintenance engineer (janitor) to the new associate you just hired, all your staff members have written duties that explain what they are expected to do.

As author Jeff Olson says, simple disciplines like this are "easy to do and easy not to do." Wouldn't you rather have your office staff working the way you want than how they think the work should get done?

Why it's done this way: Take 45 minutes to write a position contract for your new employee, and you will then have a contract that governs that employee's work, and you will spend less time worrying whether the work is being done the way you want it to be done.

But a Position Contract Is Not Enough

Okay, you've got a position contract signed and sitting in front of your new secretary's desk. Everything's copacetic, right? Not quite. You will have to monitor the work that your new secretary or paralegal is doing.

You should have your new secretary write a one-page summary of her work every week. The one-page weekly work summary doesn't have to spell out hour by hour what the secretary did (although that's a good idea), but you have to get a good sense of what work is being done. Whether it is the scheduling of depositions, the drafting of discovery responses, or meeting with new clients, you need to know what your new employee is doing.

Ask your new employee to give you a weekly work summary on Friday at 5:00 p.m. and review the work summary to make sure your goals and assignments are getting done. Look, your new secretary may gripe about the weekly work summary, but if so, is that someone you really want working for you?

Why it's done this way: You want to hold your staff (and yourself) accountable when mistakes happen or work doesn't get done the way it should. A position contract for your employees only takes an hour or two, but it removes any question or doubt as to who is responsible for doing what. You will never again hear a staff member say, "I didn't know that was my responsibility. I thought Suzy was going to do that."

14

THREE SIMPLE RULES FOR RUTHLESSLY MANAGING YOUR TIME

"What one thing could you do in your personal and professional life that, if you did on a regular basis, would make a tremendous positive difference in your life?"

—STEPHEN R. COVEY, *The 7 Habits of Highly Effective People*

WE'VE ALL HAD THESE DAYS. You get to work with a specific plan in place and soon enough, unexpected time bombs hit your plate. It might be the lawyer friend who just wants to "take a second to pick your mind," a friend from law school who wants to talk fantasy football, or perhaps the needy client who only needs your ear for a second. Either way, you get sidetracked and before you know it, 4:00 p.m. rolls around and you haven't accomplished a damn thing.

Did you have a *productive* day? Keep in mind, *being busy is not the same as being productive.* Just being busy doesn't mean a damn thing. But how do you serve your clients and get work done at the same time?

> *"It's not enough to be busy. So are the ants. The question is: what are you busy about?"*
>
> —HENRY DAVID THOREAU

First, you need to develop a system for communicating with clients. And no, a system does not include taking all phone calls as they come in. The system for client communication must be in writing and preferably signed by your clients at the first meeting. If your clients are informed about your rules for communication at your first meeting and sign an agreement that they will live by your rules, you've taken the first step to managing your time ruthlessly.

The First (and Most Important) Rule for Client Communication: No Unscheduled or Unplanned Phone Calls

This is a big one. If you continue taking unscheduled phone calls from clients (or anyone else for that matter), you will have *no control* over your time. As soon as the next phone call comes in, you will be sidetracked and redirected to a different case and a new client. This is a complete waste of your time!

You must educate new clients at your first meeting that you will not accept unscheduled phone calls. But this does not mean you will not provide access to your clients—you will, but only on your terms and when you are available.

My three rules of communication require that clients schedule a phone call with me between 4:00 p.m. and 5:30 p.m. and send a handwritten fax to me that sets forth the purpose of the phone call.

The fax will serve two important purposes: (1) it requires the clients to give careful thought to the topics that they want to discuss with me, and (2) it will give me the opportunity to be prepared for the phone call. Instead of telling the clients, "I will have to get back to you," I will have answers for the clients' questions during the phone call.

Instead of taking unscheduled phone calls, you are blocking out time to take phone calls at the end of the day *after* you've got a lot of work done. Now you are taking back control of your workday, and that's a beautiful thing.

The Second Ruthless Rule: Never Meet with Clients Who Show Up at Your Office without an Appointment

Never meet or speak with clients who show up at your office without an appointment! You need to be crystal clear with your new clients by educating them that if they show up at your office without an appointment, you will not meet or speak with them. It's that simple.

Taking time to meet with clients who do not have an appointment is even worse than taking unscheduled phone calls. If you take these unscheduled appointments, you are completely redirecting your attention and time away from the important work projects that will make money for you.

So how do you keep clients happy? You just need to explain that you will be happy to meet with them, *but only on your terms and when you are available.* Your clients must schedule a time to meet with you and send a fax listing the topics that they want to discuss at the meeting. You can allot as much time as the clients want for the meeting and you will be prepared to answer their questions. Sounds like a productive meeting, right?

The Third Ruthless Rule for Managing Your Time: Kill the E-mail Monster!

It is awfully tempting to take a break in the workday to check e-mail. Hell, e-mail is fun to read and an easy distraction from your real work. But e-mail is the ultimate time thief.

So here's what you do. Tell your new clients that you do not respond to e-mail. It is just way too easy to get caught up in responding to e-mail and convincing yourself at the end of the day that you got a lot done. You're kidding yourself!

Here's how I kill the e-mail monster: I do not open my e-mail until 12:00 noon and 4:00 p.m. each day. That's right. Why? Don't I need to stay informed of what's going on? Hell, no!

By the end of the day, the "emergencies" and the "top priority" e-mails will all have worked themselves out and usually there is no need to respond to them. But trust me. This will be the hardest thing for you to do. The habit of reading and responding to e-mail is so well engrained in us that it seems impossible to break.

But give it a shot! You will be amazed at how productive you can be when you stop taking unscheduled phone calls and unplanned office visits, and perhaps most important of all, stop reading and responding to e-mails as they hit your inbox.

The First Step to Implementing Your Rules of Communication

I ask new clients to sign a seven-page agreement that sets forth my rules, and yes, they initial each page and sign the final page to confirm they will live by my rules. There is even a page in "The Three Rules of Communication" that explains what happens if they violate the rules, including termination of the attorney-client relationship. Ouch! (But that has only happened once and I was glad to see that client go.)

Your clients should leave your first meeting with a signed copy of "The Three Rules of Communication" and an oath that they will live by them. Once you establish the ground rules, you will be amazed at how infrequently your clients will violate you rules.

At the end of the day, will your clients leave you for another lawyer? Will your clients grumble that you are not accessible to them? Well, if this happens, rip up the rules and go back to the old-school way of doing things. But I think you will be shocked at the results and how you've just managed to take back control of your time.

Turn Off Your Damn Cell Phone

Cell phones suck! Yes, I am not a fan of iPhones or the latest whiz-bang technology. For the most part, cell phones just provide another source of interruption.

And what really sucks about cell phones is they give your friends and family instant access to you. So, what can you do? *Turn the damn cell phone off!*

Are the text messages and instant messaging from your secretary really that important? (They're not.) So, here's what you can do: leave a voice message on your cell phone alerting callers that you only answer your messages at 4:00 p.m. each day and they should not expect a response from you before 4:00 p.m.

Get your clients and staff to live by your rules instead of reacting to the mindless interruptions created by cell phones, e-mails, and unscheduled phone calls!

How You Can Avoid the *Time Vampires*

Time vampires are the staff members or coworkers who just "want to pick your brain for a second." Yeah, you know who they are: the staff members who promise they will "just take a second." Half an hour later you are left wondering what happened.

The interruptions from time vampires range from meaning-less stuff such as fantasy football or the latest about the elections in Guam—just mindless chit-chat that just wastes your time.

You need to take two steps to avoid the time vampires:

1. **Close your door**. But take it one step further: tell everyone in your office that you have a "closed door policy"—namely, if your door is closed, you do not want any interruptions, not even to discuss the weather.

2. **Establish the ground rules with coworkers**. When coworkers ignore your rules (and just barge into your office) and ask for "just a second of your time," you say the following: "I'm busy right now, but I will give you all the time you need at 4:30 p.m. today. Does that work for you?" Your staff member will say, "But I just need a second," but you have to be firm with your rules.

Guaranteed: your staff members will not want to see you at 4:30 p.m. and you know why? That's right, their question was not really important in the first place. Voila! You just saved yourself from the time vampires.

Don't Knock This until You Try It: *The Value of a Cave*

Do you want a foolproof secret that will make you instantly productive? Here's a little secret: find a place where no one can find you. (I like the Albany Law School Library—I didn't go to school there, but no one seems to care.) Bring your files and turn off your cell phone. With no phone calls, text messages, e-mails, or interruptions from staff or coworkers, voilà! You just became instantly productive.

"If they can't find you, they can't interrupt you."

—DAN KENNEDY, *No B.S. Time Management for Entrepreneurs*

I recently spent 10 ½ hours of *uninterrupted* work time in my cave (actually a cubicle in the law school library, but "cave" just sounds better)—in a single day. You have got to try this!

It is amazing how much work you can do without any interruptions. *But you have to get away from the office.* It just won't work to ask your staff members to avoid interrupting you. They will, and even if they don't, it's just too easy to get distracted by phone calls and time vampires asking you about last night's Yankees' game.

My time in a cave is easily the best and most productive use of my time.

Force Yourself to Spend 80 Percent of Your Time on Your Five Best Cases

Stephen R. Covey's *The 7 Habits of Highly Effective People* is a must read, and I love his third habit, "Put First Things First." The essence of Covey's third habit is: *Things that matter the most must never be at the mercy of things that matter the least.*

For lawyers, Covey's third habit can be restated as: "Work on the cases that will make the most money and ignore the rest." Yes, make a list of your top five cases and focus on them over all others (even if that means neglecting your other cases).

I call my top cases the A cases and ask my team to focus on those cases over all others. Time management (or self-management, as Covey calls it) won't get you anywhere if you are spending your time on the wrong cases.

The *One Question* You Should Ask throughout Your Workday

Here's a question you should always ask (at least every hour through your workday), "Can someone else do the work that I am about to do?" If the answer is "Yeah, my secretary can do this," stop what you are doing and give the damn task to your secretary.

If you can delegate a task, you must delegate it. I know, it's so easy to say, "Yeah, but I can do this faster" or maybe, "I can do this better." No, no, no! If the task can be delegated, you cannot do it—that's if you ever want to get things done and see your family for dinner every once in a while.

Be brutally honest with yourself by asking, "What are the things that only I can do?" Don't even start a new task without thinking, "Can my paralegal or secretary do this?" I'll bet there's a good chance they can and that means, stop working and delegate the job.

As a malpractice trial lawyer, there are certain things I can't delegate such as trials and depositions. But I'm really not that indispensable or important to virtually anything else. Just about everything else from preparing discovery responses and bills of particulars to responding to e-mail and meeting with clients can be done by my team members (in this case a world-class paralegal, Corina Skidmore). And guess what? The same is true for you.

Hey, I was the worst offender not long ago. That's right, I had to be "the guy." I had to be the one to answer client phone calls and respond immediately to the flurry of e-mails from clients and defense lawyers. (Oh yeah, I was convinced that I was so important to my clients.) What a huge waste of time! And let's face it, did clients really insist that I personally answer every phone call or respond to their e-mails? Hell, no (and you should fire your clients if they are that bossy).

You have to get over the idea that you are indispensable to your clients. You're not serving your clients by running around in fifteen different directions.

15

HOW YOU CAN CRUSH THE E-MAIL TIME VAMPIRE

"Time is the most precious asset any entrepreneur possesses."

—DAN KENNEDY, *No B.S. Time Management for Entrepreneurs*

EACH DAY WE ARE INUNDATED with e-mails that are pointless. All it takes is just one person to click on "Reply to All" and a monster is created. All of a sudden half of your office is sending you a string of pointless reply-to-all e-mails and swamping your e-mail box with completely meaningless, silly e-mails. You delete the string of e-mails (I don't bother reading them), but why should you even have to?

Kill the reply-to-all e-mail monster with one simple rule: Tell your staff that they should reply only to the primary sender of the e-mail. *Never hit the Reply to All button.* To make things simple, end your e-mails with, "To save time, please reply only to me rather than hitting the Reply to All button." Better yet, avoid group e-mail altogether.

Ed Wilcenski, Esq., an elder law attorney in Clifton Park, New York, has a unique solution to the reply-to-all monster. Ed has a simple rule: unless an e-mail requires his response, he should not be copied on e-mails. Let me give it to you straight from Ed:

> I recently implemented a system whereby my staff is not permitted to copy me on e-mail messages unless my review or response is required. Instead, I block off a half a day each week and give the staff an opportunity to meet with me without interruption. They are expected to prepare an agenda in advance.

I love the concept of restrictions on e-mail and weekly meetings with staff meetings with the submission of a written agenda before the meeting. This is a beautiful time saver that gives your team face-to-face time with you on a weekly basis with an agenda that almost guarantees a productive meeting. No one complains. You've got happy campers and killed the e-mail reply-to-all monster.

This is advanced stuff! But even Ed isn't quite ready for my methods for killing e-mail: "I'm not quite sure I'm ready to leave my Outlook program off for half a day, but I may experiment with variations on the theme."

Hey, no one's perfect. But Ed is not alone. When lawyers read my "Three Rules of Communication" that limits clients' access to me, their response is the same: "Sounds great, but that would never work for me." Or perhaps, "I pride myself on giving my clients access to me." (You don't think I've heard this before do you?)

Come on! How do you know that my rules of communication won't work for you if you've never tried them? Look, you just have to get your clients to buy into your rules of communication from your first meeting with them, and once you've reached an agreement, they'll understand the steps that they must take to meet or speak with you. Just explain one thing: "You will always have access to me, *but when my schedule permits.*"

How to Kill Useless Thank-You E-mails

Everyone wants to be polite, but the trivial thank-you e-mails that swamp your e-mail inbox are pointless interruptions to your day. Kill the thank-you e-mails with a heavy dose of the acronym, NRN in the subject line of your e-mails. NRN means "**N**o **r**eply is **n**eeded," or even better, use NTN, an acronym for "**N**o **t**hanks **n**eeded." You just killed the trivial thank-you e-mails in one fell swoop.

Let's face it: e-mail is greatly overused and wastes a ton of your time every day. The simple rule of thumb is "send less, receive less." Remember, *being busy is not the same as being productive.*

Aggressively Unsubscribe from List Serves and Group E-mail Lists

It's always tempting to answer list serve questions to serve our fellow members of the bar. Hey, we've worked hard to acquire these fancy degrees and sometimes we want to show off our knowledge. As New Yorkers say, forget about it!

Aggressively unsubscribe for all of your list serves. Sure, it's great to help out fellow lawyers by answering their questions, but this is a complete waste of your time. List serves and group e-mails are just another pointless distraction in the course of your day. Make sure you remove this distraction whenever a new, unwanted e-mail pops up in Microsoft Outlook by unsubscribing from list serves and group e-mails.

Have Your Secretary Check and Clear Your e-Mail Twice a Day

What if you never had to read e-mail again? Guess what? You can just by having your secretary or paralegal check and clear your e-mail twice a day.

Experiment with removing yourself from e-mail completely by giving your secretary carte blanche to answer your e-mail. Rather than spending two to three hours a day reading and responding to e-mail, let your secretary do this at predetermined times during the day, say 11 a.m. and 3 p.m.

Just explain to your secretary that you want her to filter through your e-mails, respond to as many of the e-mails as she can, and then mark the e-mails that you need to see. Tell your secretary to use her judgment (you trust her by now, right?) and get rid of as many of the e-mails as possible.

If an e-mail absolutely requires your response, it's no big deal. Just having your secretary mark the e-mails as "action items" that require your response and voila! You just made roughly 90 percent of the e-mails vanish from your inbox.

Just Say No to E-mail

The best step you can take *today* is to stop checking e-mail in the morning. Better yet, don't even open Microsoft Outlook until at least noon.

Reading and responding to e-mail serves almost no purpose other than wasting your time. But e-mail is a welcome distraction to productive work, so when that little box pops up in the lower right corner of your computer screen, you are tempted to read and respond to the new e-mail. Just say no!

By the time you read and respond to the new e-mail, you've just wasted 20 minutes, and by the way, what were you even doing when you got the e-mail? By the time you figure out what you were doing before the e-mail, you've wasted half an hour.

Here's a solution for you: *do not open your e-mail until noon* (this means closing out of Outlook completely).

This is really hard to do for e-mail junkies (I confess that used to be me) and you won't be perfect, but give this a shot. You will be amazed at how much more productive you will be. You will dedicate your morning to productive work on your top cases. Damn, it feels great when you spend two hours of completely uninterrupted work time on your "A" cases.

When I am in the office, I avoid the craving to read e-mail by shutting down Microsoft Outlook. I do not scan or read e-mail until noon (at the earliest) and I try to avoid reading e-mail until 4:00 p.m. In the afternoon, I close out Outlook until 4:00 p.m. Yeah, it's hard sometimes and I'm not perfect. But you will not believe how much more productive you will be once you *just say no to e-mail.*

16

SETTING YOUR GOALS IN CONCRETE

"Goals that are not written down are just wishes."

—FITZHUGH DODSON

THE MOST OVERLOOKED ASPECT of any law firm is *goal setting*. Law firms, both big and small, practice without any goals whatsoever. No financial goals, no goals for each case—no goals, period. Big mistake!

Where are you heading? If you have no path, you will be reactionary and directionless. Have a clear picture of the future. What do you want your law firm to be like in three years, five years?

First, three simple rules about goal setting:

1. Goals must be *specific*.

2. Goals must have a *deadline*.

3. Goals must be *written down and regularly reviewed*.

What is a surefire sign of a winner? Someone who has the goals written down and in his possession at all times. So here's a tip that will put you miles ahead of your peers: Write your goals down; laminate them for keepsake purposes; put your goal reminder in your wallet, and once a day, review your goals. By doing this one simple thing, you will be head and shoulders above every other lawyer in your town.

> **"When you set your objectives for the year, you record them in concrete."**
>
> —JIM COLLINS, *Good to Great*

Seems easy to do, right? But it's also easy not to do (to borrow Jeff Olson's phrase from *The Slight Edge*).

Your goals should be divided into at least four categories: money (budget/income), marketing, operations, and personal. Each goal must have three things:

- Goal: What you want to accomplish—namely, your primary objective;

- Plan: how you intend to accomplish the goal;

- Daily discipline: what you can do every day to accomplish the goal—namely, the little tiny things you do every day that slowly move you forward to reaching your goal. You must have one daily discipline that you will commit to doing every day to advance your goal.

If you're like every other lawyer, you just don't have time to write down your goals. But *goal setting is what separates the winners from the dreamers.* There is no technical work that you can do for your law firm that is more important than goal setting.

> **"If you don't stay focused on your goals, you will spend your life achieving the objectives of other people—particularly those who are goal-oriented."**
>
> —GRANT CARDONE, *The 10X Rule*

Just as you would set aside one hour to meet with an important client, you have to have integrity with yourself. So, try this: just schedule one hour today to create your goals. And treat that one hour as if it is an appointment in court that you must attend—in other words, be on time and be fully committed to spending the hour on your goals. There is no better use of your time than goal setting.

Money Goals (Budget/Income)

> **"Most small businesses fail because of poor accounting."**
>
> —DAVE RAMSEY, *EntreLeadership*

The first thing you must do is hire a bookkeeper and create a budget. Develop a budget for the law practice and put a real accounting system in place for your law firm. I don't care how small your law firm is or if you have no employees. You must *know your numbers*.

Costs of Your Law Firm

KNOW THE NUMBERS

There are two kinds of costs: fixed and variable. It should be easy for you to calculate your fixed costs on a monthly basis. Variable costs fluctuate, but you can create estimates of variable costs for every lawsuit if you *just do the math*.

- Fixed costs: Begin by getting exact figures on the fixed costs ranging from rent, malpractice insurance, payroll, phone, and Internet service to website hosting, parking, and so on.

- Variable costs: You must estimate the variable, nonfixed costs, which include office supplies, bookkeeper and accounting fees, phone answering service, expert fees, filing fees, stenographer and videographer fees.

Your spreadsheet for fixed and variable costs should be broken down by at least two categories: operating expenses and marketing expenses. Be as precise as possible. Get your staff to review your figures for fixed and variable costs. (Better yet, have your bookkeeper review the numbers.)

You can even break down the variable operating expenses between your office expenses and "work in progress." The additional category of "work in progress" refers to the ongoing expenses associated with every lawsuit, including filing fees, stenographer's and videographer's fees for depositions, expert fees, costs of medical records, travel, and so on.

PROJECTING MARKETING COSTS

You must establish the marketing costs for specific categories, including graphic design, fulfillment services (printing and mailing marketing stuff), content creation for website, audio/video production, lawyers seminars/workshops, appreciation parties, website, book publishing, advertising, direct mail costs, and automated follow-up with new leads (e.g., Infusionsoft).

RETAINED PROFITS

Your goal should be to have at least six months of operating capital saved in cash. Every time you receive a legal fee, put a percentage of the profits aside as retained earnings. When you build liquidity with retained earnings, you can weather any storm.

BUSINESS V. PERSONAL EXPENSES

You shouldn't use your personal finances to pay business expenses, and you shouldn't use your business account to pay personal expenses. Run your law firm like the great business that it is.

Income of Your Law Firm

PROJECTING FUTURE INCOME

In the budget for your law firm, you must project future income and expenses and thus profits. The best way to project income is based upon estimated minimum legal fees expected to be received in a calendar year from your cases that have firm trial dates during that year. If you don't have a trial date, you can't expect to get your legal fee that year.

When projecting future income, you should use a conservative projection for the resolution of each of your cases. It's always better to have more money coming in than you expected.

The income and expense sheet should have a realistic projection of your anticipated profit. You should project your numbers at least 24 months into the future.

REVIEWING THE NUMBERS WITH YOUR STAFF

On the first Monday of every month, you should have a 15-minute meeting on the financial reports and income projections. I share the financial numbers with my staff, even how much I have in the bank. By giving your staff complete access to your financial numbers, you will strengthen their commitment to your firm and they will be far more likely to take an ownership mentality.

> **"It's the ability to generate commitment in others that dictates the ultimate path of the business."**
>
> —JOHN JANTSCH, *The Commitment Engine*

The monthly meeting is a good way to keep your staff on track with your financial goals and let them see firsthand how their work is impacting your firm's bottom line. But most of all, this is a unique way of doing business that no other law firm in your town (or your state) is doing. This alone separates your firm from every other law firm and this uniqueness will set you apart with prospective employees.

Profit Goals

You must set goals for the amount of money you intend to make. The key point is to have a number that you are pointing to, and to get your staff members on board with your profit goals.

But here's the key thing: you can't set vague, unrealistic goals. This is pointless! Don't set a profit goal of $2 million for next year if you know that goal is completely unrealistic and unattainable in the short term.

Set goals that are realistic, smart, and time bound. Let's say that after preparing your income and expense projections, you project a modest income. That's fine. Let's work from there. Let's set a goal of increasing your net income by 25 percent per year for each successive year. So, even if your net income, or profit, is relatively modest, you set realistic goals to increase your income every year for three years.

And put precise numbers on the financial goals. Be as specific as possible in projecting income for each of the next three years and set a specific date for when you intend to reach each of your profit goals.

"Fix in your mind the exact amount of money you deserve."

—Napoleon Hill, *Think & Grow Rich*

Then show the numbers to your staff and get them on board with your goals. If you want your staff to buy into your goals, you can't expect to get where you want if your team doesn't know where you're heading.

Marketing Goals

"Begin by quantifying everything related to how you do business."

—Michael E. Gerber, *The E-Myth Revisited*

How many new case calls/clients did you receive in the last 12 months? What was the source of those new case calls? How do you know whether your marketing is working if you don't know these answers?

The marketing plan should be measured by four categories:

- Number of *total* new case calls: Every single new case call must be entered in the Intake Wizard in Trialworks.

- Number of new *rejected* cases: The number of new case calls that resulted in a rejection letter on the first day the new client called your law firm. This will be the majority of new case calls.

- Number of new *potential* cases: The number of new case calls that had enough merit to evaluate the merit of the case after the initial phone call with the new client. The case may have questionable merit, but based upon the damages, it is worth a review of the medical records. The case should be moved to the Under Consideration tab in Trialworks. Cases that are "under consideration" are *potential* cases.

- Number of new *active* cases: The number of new case calls that result in the filing of a lawsuit—namely, an "active" case. The number of active cases is typically a very low number.

All of the new case calls should be tracked in your case management software program. There should not be a single new client whose contact information is not entered into your case management software program. Otherwise, it will be impossible to track the number of new case calls and what happened with each case.

Again, set realistic goals for marketing—not pie in the sky goals that you know you can't achieve. Let's say you received 453 new case calls last year and you set a goal of an additional 20 percent of new case calls for each of the next three years. Now you can put specific numbers on your goals for new case calls over the next three years.

In year one, your goal is to have 90 additional new case calls or a total of 543; in year two, your goal is to have an additional 108 new case calls or a total of 651; and in year three, your goal is to have an additional 130 new case calls or a total of 781. Over the course of three years, you went from a total of 453 new case calls to 781. That's an increase of 328 new case calls per year.

If a 20 percent increase is not realistic, set a more realistic goal such as 10 percent or even 5 percent. You'll be tempted to project lofty goals, but if the goals were never realistic or attainable in the first place, your goals will be meaningless.

MARKETING GOALS ON STEROIDS

Try to quantify everything you can. You should have marketing goals for:

- number of referrals

- number of first-time referral partners (lawyers who refer new cases to you)

- number of unique website visitors by month

- number of new cases generated by the website

- number of testimonials on website or avvo.com from clients and referral partners

But it's pointless if you're just documenting the numbers. You have to review the numbers, preferably quarterly, to determine whether you're on track to meet your marketing goals.

Operating Goals (Case Management)

"In the absence of standards, your life will drift aimlessly, without purpose, without meaning."

—MICHAEL E. GERBER, *The E-Myth Revisited*

You should put targets and deadlines on different aspects of every lawsuit. Each lawsuit should have a budget and targeted goals for each of the four phases of the lawsuit. Chapter 11 ("The Key Performance Indicators for Success") sets forth specific standards for each of the four phases of a lawsuit.

But it's not enough to simply have goals for each case. You must write them down. I prefer a flow chart for each case that documents the number of days that it took for each phase of the lawsuit. Next to the actual number of days for a phase of the lawsuit, you should have the goal stated on your flow chart and difference between the actual number of days that it took to complete a phase of the lawsuit and the number of days set forth in your goal.

At the end of each lawsuit, the flow chart should be completed by your staff member so you can gauge how you performed relative to your operating goals. Hey, even with a great settlement, you may not be accomplishing your goals if the case took too long to get to trial.

Personal Goals (Your "One, Big Audacious Goal")

"With no picture of how you wish your life to be, how on earth can you begin to live it?"

—MICHAEL E. GERBER, *The E-Myth Revisited*

True success is your legacy and the impact that you have on the world. Why is the world different as a result of your being here? How would you describe the overall value or meaning of your life? After you leave this world, will you leave behind a legacy?

Make your goals *huge*. Use a dream board to list your lifetime goals—your 100-year goals. Write your dreams down, make them specific and give them a concrete timeline for realization.

*"The difference between great people and everyone
else is that great people create their lives' activities
while everyone else is created by their lives, passively
waiting to see where life takes them next."*

—MICHAEL E. GERBER, *The E-Myth Revisited*

Dream of things that you are passionate about and take one small step every day toward the realization of this goal. Let's say you want to help the parents of handicapped children by providing resources and information to them. Great! Begin by creating a plan. Be specific and put your plan in writing. Take daily steps—even tiny ones— toward your goal and make progress, if not every day, then every week toward your goal.

Weekly Goals: Think of one or two important results you feel you should accomplish during the next seven days. These would be recorded as goals. Now you can look at the week ahead with your goals in mind and schedule time to achieve them.

*"'Time management' is really a misnomer—the challenge
is not to manage time, but to manage ourselves."*

—STEPHEN R. COVEY, *The 7 Habits of Highly Effective People*

Give yourself something to work toward constantly. Begin each day on a disciplined schedule. Each day look at what you are committed to accomplishing. You should begin and finish each day by writing goals down and reviewing them.

Practice tip: Print your goals on a laminated sheet of paper that you keep in your wallet and review them daily. Plan each day and prioritize your activities.

17

HOW TO HIRE YOUR NEXT SUPERSTAR EMPLOYEE

"Those who build great companies understand that the ultimate throttle on growth for any great company is not markets, or technology, or competition, or products. It is one thing above all others: the ability to get and keep enough of the right people."

—JIM COLLINS, *Good to Great*

IT'S SO TEMPTING to take the easy way out. When it comes to hiring a new employee, it's just so easy to take the first candidate who has a nice smile, appears motivated, and seems somewhat bright. Hey, you've got a ton of work to do, and the hiring process is getting in the way of your real work. The temptation is to just hire the first person and get it over with, but there's one big problem: *interviews mean nothing.*

That's right. You can't tell a damn thing from an interview. All candidates come to their interview wearing their Sunday finest, beaming smiles and puppy-dog enthusiasm. You leave the interview convinced that you just discovered the next great secretary or paralegal for your law firm. The honeymoon begins when you hire your new employee and everything seems to move along just swimmingly.

But then a funny thing happens. Your new superstar employee starts showing up a few minutes late to work a couple of times and before you know it, she is leaving work five minutes early. You shrug this off as an aberration in the stubborn hope you made the right choice. But time slowly and surely leaves you with no doubt that your "superstar" employee is a train wreck. But what can you do now?

It's hard. You want to be well liked by your staff and firing an employee is never pleasant. So, like everyone else, you find ways to put off the inevitable decision to fire. Maybe it's Christmas and you just don't want to be Scrooge. And deep inside, you are still hoping your new secretary makes a miraculous comeback and a strong work ethic will magically appear out of thin air.

But you know that you're kidding yourself. Things won't change. In fact, they'll get worse.

So Why Is It So Damn Hard to Fire the New Employee?

It's simple: you don't want to have to go through the interview process all over again. You dread the interview process more than anything and you know, even with the best interviews imaginable, you can't tell anything from an interview. So, what can you do? Throw up your hands and give up?

One *Big* Confession

Your systems and rules in your law firm *cannot* mold a bad employee into a good employee. It doesn't matter who you are. If you've got the wrong person for the job, there's not a damn thing you can do about it. Inevitably, you will be forced to fire the new employee or she will quit, but either way, the outcome will be bad for all.

The goal is simple: finding the right people who will not require constant discipline and supervision to do the job, the kind of people who will do the job even when no one is watching and take pride in getting the job done right. You know whom we're talking about: employees who come early to work and leave late and show up on weekends when they are behind in their work. More than anything else, the right employees are those who take an *ownership attitude* to the work. They are *invested in their work* and you don't need to stand over their shoulder to make sure the job gets done.

"The best people don't need to be managed."

—JIM COLLINS, *Good to Great*

I know what you're thinking. The superstar employee doesn't exist in my town. That's right. Your town just happens to be the worst place in the world for finding legal secretaries and paralegals. But guess what? You're wrong!

But How Do You Find the Superstar Employee?

Great legal secretaries and paralegals are everywhere, including in your town. You just have to find them. But you already know that the interview is meaningless, and if you've seen one resume, you've seen them all. So what can you do to find the superstar employee?

THREE SIMPLE STEPS TO HIRING A SUPERSTAR EMPLOYEE

Have you ever thought what little time and effort go into the advertisements for secretaries and paralegals? One advertisement looks identical to the next: "AV-rated law firm seeks legal secretary with three to five years of experience in personal injury." Blah, blah, blah. What crap!

Why would a superstar secretary want to interview at a law firm that sounds like just another ordinary firm? So you jazz things up a bit. In your advertisement you state that your firm offers a *"golden opportunity* for personal growth and development that places the utmost value on *you."* Wow! You just got readers' attention.

But don't stop there. Your advertisement must spell out specifically how you are different from every other law firm, and yes, that includes fully paid health insurance for spouse and family, a salary that is the highest in the legal community, and three weeks of paid vacation. Oh, and before you forget, you offer training and education in personal development and growth—for example, Dale Carnegie, which has nothing to do with the law.

Now the prospective secretaries' heads are spinning. The secretarial candidates are ready to knock down your door to get an interview. You've got the interest of a whole bunch of candidates, but how do you pick the right one?

THE SECOND STEP TO FINDING THE SUPERSTAR EMPLOYEE

Now that you've got a boatload of candidates for the position, you've got to weed them out before the interview. You want to make it as difficult as possible to apply for the position. In your advertisement, you explain that candidates must follow a sequence of steps in order to be considered for the position, and if they fail to comply to the "T" with your instructions, their resumes will be thrown in the waste basket.

Your advertisement should require that the candidates submit a cover letter with the subject line, "Why I Am the Perfect Candidate to Be Your Secretary," together with a resume, and names and addresses of three references (whom you will not contact without the candidate's permission). Your advertisement should explicitly require the candidates to send the written materials via Federal Express (not UPS or other overnight delivery carriers) and leave a voice message on a specially designated phone service, explaining why they are perfect for the job. In your advertisement, you should explain that you will not accept phone calls, walk-ins, or e-mails, and the candidates will instantly be disqualified from consideration if they do not follow your instructions.

If 100 candidates apply, how many do you think will comply with your rules? Less than one-third. Some will try to contact you with phone calls or e-mails and others will fail to sign the cover letter or forget to provide references. You should review the cover letter and resume for grammatical errors. It never fails that almost every resume or cover letter has at least one grammatical mistake.

And that's just fine because *you don't want to waste time interviewing candidates who cannot follow simple instructions or are careless about following instructions.* If they can't follow your simple instructions when applying for the job, how do you think they're going to do once they've got the position?

You've just weeded out two-thirds of the candidates before conducting a single interview.

A CRUCIAL THIRD STEP IN THE HIRING PROCESS
THAT IS ALMOST ALWAYS IGNORED

So you've weeded out two-thirds of the candidates and you're left with some excellent candidates—at least on paper. What can you do before the interviews to find the right candidate? It seems simple, but very few employers check references. First, ask for the candidates' permission to contact their references and then call every reference listed by the candidates on their application.

You may be shocked by the results. It's amazing what references will say about the candidate—and it's not always complimentary.

People listed as references may hem and haw about the candidate and give a lukewarm assessment, and now you know this isn't one of the candidates you want to interview.

You can find out a lot more about the candidate from the references than you can tell from looking at a piece of paper (the resume) or spending 20 minutes, speaking with the candidate in your office. Now that you've narrowed down the field to three to four candidates, it's time for the interview.

A Unique Approach to Interviews (and Something the Candidates Never Expected)

If you are interviewing secretaries or receptionists, have them answer the phone during the interview. Let the candidates show you what they've got. You can learn a lot just from a couple of phone calls with the candidates in the office setting. Do they smile when they answer the phone? Do they follow your phone script? Are they kind and compassionate with your clients?

If you like certain candidates, let your staff interview them and give you their evaluation. It might not be the same as yours. And if your staff members don't care for the selected candidates, you can't hire them. *Your staff should always have the ultimate veto power with new hires* because they will spend more time with them than you will.

And always keep in mind one cardinal principle:

"When in doubt, don't hire—keep looking ... You absolutely must have the discipline not to hire until you find the right people"

Jim Collins, *Good to Great*

As the adage says, "Fire fast, hire slow." Take your time in the hiring process and if you're not sure about a candidate, take more time. It's a pain interviewing more candidates, but just think of the alternative: you will spend the next six months with a secretary who doesn't show up on time and can't follow your office rules, and whom, after the six months, you have to fire. And you start the whole process over again.

Remember, nothing you can do will turn the wrong people into the right people.

The Ultimate Goal: Self-Disciplined, Committed Employees

What is your goal? To find a new secretary or paralegal that you couldn't imagine living without. Once you've found that person, overpay her big time, and you'll never have to do another interview.

"It all starts with disciplined people. The transition begins not by trying to discipline the wrong people into the right behaviors, but by getting self-disciplined people on the bus in the first place."

—JIM COLLINS, *Good to Great*

Once you get the right people on board, you won't have to worry whether they will show up on time and do the work that you ask. Self-disciplined staff members who are committed to the culture of your business don't have to be told what to do … and you won't have to worry about interviewing the next round of candidates.

18

HOW TO DECIDE WHETHER YOU SHOULD TAKE THE CASE

(JUST MAKE SURE YOU *DO THE MATH* BEFORE YOU ACCEPT YOUR NEXT CASE)

HAVE YOU EVER REGRETTED accepting a case—sometimes just after you sign the retainer agreement? There could be a million reasons: maybe your client is a contract killer for the mob, a cross-dressing crack addict, or spent 15 years in prison for defrauding the mentally handicapped (yes, these are just a few of my clients). But more often than not, you second-guess your decision to accept the case because, in hindsight, you reach the conclusion that it *just wasn't worth it*.

Now, c'mon, you know what I mean. We've all been there. You accept the case with rose-colored lenses on and dream of a big pay day, but pretty soon you start seeing the blemishes in the case. A lot of times the bad news snowballs, and then you wish you had never taken the case, but by that time it's too late. You signed a retainer agreement and filed the lawsuit, so there's no backing out now.

But here's a tip: before you sign the retainer agreement and file the lawsuit, set aside one hour to *do the math* so you know whether the case is worth your time before you file the lawsuit.

There are three simple steps to determine whether you should take the case. By following these three steps, you will know whether case is worth taking *before* you file the lawsuit.

STEP #1: Every Case That You Should Accept Should Have a Budget

You begin by estimating the expenses for each phase of the lawsuit. I break the categories into three phases: (1) the discovery phase from commencement of the lawsuit until the filing of the note of issue, (2) the trial preparation phase from the filing of the note of issue until the first day of the trial, and (3) the trial phase that begins on day one of the trial until the conclusion of the case.

Each of the three phases will have their own budgets. In the discovery phase, the budget includes the expenses for filing fees, stenographer's and videographer's fees for depositions, and expert fees for reviewing the case. The budget in the discovery phase includes a list of all depositions that you intend to conduct, including the name of every witness to be deposed and the estimated cost of each deposition.

The budget for the trial preparation phase consists mostly of expert fees for reviewing deposition transcripts, meetings with experts, the costs of pretrial exhibits (with *great* trial exhibit experts such as Mark Whalen of Litigraphics, LLC in Baldwinsville, NY), and in some cases, fees for mediation.

The trial phase will include a budget for expert fees for trial testimony, and the costs of travel and hotels for the expert witnesses. If you intend to get transcripts of trial testimony, include an estimate for this expense. You don't have to be perfect with your estimates, but you should try to be as precise as possible, and you should always err on the high side of the estimate just to be safe.

Let's say you estimate that the cost of the discovery phase will be $13,445 (but be as precise and specific as you can), the cost of the trial preparation phase will be $6,170, and the costs of the trial phase will be $17,222. So, now you have an estimate for the total cost of the lawsuit of $36,837. Great, but you're just getting started.

Now, I know what you're thinking: *how can I estimate the costs for the trial when I accept the case?* Well, you can't. But you can put ball-park estimates on the costs for all three phases of the lawsuit before you sign the retainer agreement if you sit down and map out a game plan for the case—namely, estimate the number of depositions and expert witnesses.

Let's say you will need a neurologist, neuropsychologist, life care planner, and an economist for a case involving a brain injured child. Okay, now estimate the fees for the physical examination of the medical experts, the retainer for the review of the file, and the fee for meeting with you and testifying at the trial. See, that wasn't so bad. Now you've got some numbers to work with.

STEP #2: Placing a Value on the Case

Are you done yet? Not quite, so stay with me.

You have to put a dollar number on the value of the case before you sign the retainer agreement or file the lawsuit. At the beginning of the case, you don't need a figure for the settlement demand, but you will need a number for the settlement value. As I mentioned earlier, the settlement value of the case is the absolute lowest number that you will recommend for settlement (aka bottom line).

Let's say you accept a wrongful death case involving the death of a 41-year-old mother who was married and had two children. You estimate the pecuniary damages under New York's wrongful death statute for loss of earnings, loss of household services, and loss of maternal guidance, nurturing, and advice. Once you have an estimate for the pecuniary damages, you estimate the noneconomic damages consisting of conscious pain and suffering. For argument sake, let's say you project the total damages at $2 million.

Next, you have to face a stark reality: yes, you might lose the case (don't kid yourself if you think you can't lose). Let's say that you conservatively estimate that there is a 50/50 chance of winning on liability at trial. And just to err on the side of caution, you might want to lower the estimate to a chance of 40 percent that you win.

With a 40 percent chance of success on liability, you reduce the total damages of $2 million to $800,000 to reflect the reality that you might not win the case. Now, you have a settlement value of $800,000.

Step #3: You Must Compare the Case Expenses to Your Legal Fee to Justify Accepting the Case

Now, it's time to do the math.

First, you must calculate the legal fee on the settlement value of $800,000. After reducing the settlement by the disbursements of $36,837, the legal fee under New York's sliding scale for a medical malpractice lawsuit is $190,132.

But you're not done yet. If you have a referral partner, you will have to pay a referral fee that is 24.9 percent of the total legal fee, or $47,368. This will reduce your portion of the legal fee to $142,764. Okay, so you stand to make $142,764, based on your estimate of the cases expenses (Step #1) and the settlement value of the case (Step #2).

Now, you must compare your case budget (Step #1) to the legal fee that you expect to earn. In this example, the case expenses of $36,837 are 25.8 percent of your legal fee of $142,764. An investment of $36,837 will yield a return of $142,764. In this example, your legal fee exceeds the case disbursements by a ratio of 4 to 1 (and that's not good).

Is this case worth taking? The ideal ratio of your legal fee to case disbursements is 10 to 1. If you spend $20,000 in case disbursements, you will need a legal fee (after paying your referral partners) that is at least $200,000.

How Doing the Math Will Help You Avoid the Cases You Wish You Never Accepted

I know, I know. It's hard to get the numbers to add up in many cases. And there will always be a case or two where you want to make an exception based on principle. (I hate taking cases on principle, but I'm guilty too.) But if you do the math before you file the lawsuit and sign the retainer agreement, you just might avoid the case that you just wish you had never accepted in the first place, such as the contract killer for the mob, who calls you every 15 minutes.

THE INSIDER'S SECRET TO BUILDING A MILLION DOLLAR INJURY LAW FIRM

It takes chutzpah to build a million dollar injury law firm. Why? Because you have to turn down cases that you know are worth decent money and it's not always easy, especially when you're having a dry spell financially. It's tempting to make an exception just once or twice for cases that have limited value—either due to modest damages or marginal liability, but you have to resist the temptation.

Many lawyers with high volume personal injury practices adopt the theory that you have to take the "bad with the good" to get the occasional jewel. THEY'RE WRONG! You cannot build a million dollar injury firm by letting crappy cases through your front door. Just think, every crappy case is taking your time away from your money makers. And eventually, the crap cases will just suck your time away and make you crazy because you can't keep track of your cases.

HERE'S YOUR FORMULA FOR SUCCESS

Once you accept a new case, you must place a settlement value on the case, a.k.a. the "bottom line." Based upon the settlement value, the case will be given a Priority Code ranging from A, B, C and D. The "A" cases have a settlement value of $1,000,000 or higher, the "B" cases have a settlement value between $500,000 and $1,000,000, the "C" cases are worth between $300,000 and $500,000 and the "D" cases...well, let's hope you're not taking many "D" cases. The "D" cases are worth less than $300,000. The Priority Code for each case should be documented in the "Case/Retainer" tab of Trialworks.

You want to devote as much of your time and resources to your "A" and "B" cases. But what if you only have one or two "A" or "B" cases? No problem, my friend. I'd much rather have three "A" cases than 3,000 crappy cases. Let the other lawyers in your town fight for the scraps.

It's okay to take the "C" cases, but you better have a damn good reason for taking a "D" case—perhaps you represent a family member or your best friend's wife. But if you get in the habit of taking "D" cases, you will NEVER have a million dollar law firm. Instead, you'll be fighting to keep your head above water all day long with marginal cases.

BUT CAN YOU STILL MAKE MONEY FROM CRAPPY CASES?

Just because you decline the "D" cases doesn't mean you can't make money on them. Here's what you do: refer the "D" cases to the "young stud" lawyer in your town. Every town has a young, aggressive lawyer just chomping at the bit to get experience. Chances are this young stud lawyer will do a better job than you handling the "D" cases and the clients are better off.

You should establish a referral relationship with the young stud lawyer and monitor the cases that he handles. Now you're making referral fees from the "D" cases and the crap cases aren't consuming any of your time. It's a win-win!

If you want to handle catastrophic injury cases for a living, you must live by one cardinal rule: IT'S BETTER TO HAVE 3 CASES THAN 300 CASES! And don't worry—if you're selective and very careful in case selection, just one catastrophic injury case can pay all of your bills for the whole year.

19

HOW TO GET THE BEST SETTLEMENT FOR YOUR NEXT CASE

PICTURE THIS SCENARIO: You've toiled for years with cases that *just pay the bills,* but you've finally got the perfect case. This ideal case has everything: great liability, massive damages, and unlimited insurance coverage. The life care plan projects future medical care that will cost $20 million, and loss of earnings adds $3 million to the damages, and that's before you even get to the enormous noneconomic damages. This is the case you've been waiting for your whole career. Everything's perfect, right?

But there's a problem. The defense attorneys aren't quite playing along. Instead of acknowledging the problems with the defense case and making a settlement offer that reflects the value of the damages, the defense lawyers play games (hell, this is what they're paid to do). One week before trial, you get a low-ball offer that is not even in the ballpark of what you consider a reasonable offer. Making things worse, the defense lawyers present you with a final take-it-or-leave-it low-ball offer just before trial.

Doubts race through your mind. Perhaps you didn't evaluate the liability or damages correctly? A case that always seemed rock solid now begins to raise doubts in your mind about its true value or perhaps the phantom defense theories raised by the defense lawyers now seem real to you. You think that maybe you should fold up the tent and go home with the best settlement offer you can get.

You are faced with a dilemma. You want to go to trial, but the settlement offer is just enough to tempt you to settle. What do you do?

There is an answer. It's really simple and it works.

The Absolute Worst Thing You Can Do

The number-one mistake that injury lawyers make in settlement negotiations is to enter negotiations with the mindset of "*Let's see how we can do.*" These lawyers have no negotiation strategy, but rather, simply hope for the best settlement offer they can get.

The let's-see-how-we-can-do approach is really no strategy at all. It's a willy-nilly dreamer's approach that removes all strategy from the art of negotiating the best settlement. And yes, on occasion, it gets the result that you want, but that usually means you just had some blind luck.

While it seems inconceivable that the let's-see-how-we-can-do negotiation strategy would result in a great settlement, on occasion it does. But does this mean that this strategy (it's really not a strategy at all) will work for you in the long run? Au contraire, my friend.

This is a recipe for disaster.

You will never have control over the negotiation as long as you continue using the nonstrategy of "*Let's see how we can do.*" So, if you're with me, let's get started with a solution.

The First Thing You Should Do *before* Settlement Negotiations

Okay, so you know that the *"let's see how we can do"* is an amateur's way of negotiating a settlement. (Don't kick yourself if you've used this approach before; we all have.) But what can you do to get the best settlement possible?

Here's where you start: you need *two numbers*. You will need to determine the numbers for settlement value and the goal.

The first number is the *settlement value*. No, this is not the full value of the damages that you could get from a jury. (Stop dreaming already!) Rather, the settlement value is a number that takes into consideration the problems in your case.

Let's say you've got a case in which liability is weak and there is a strong possibility of a defense verdict. You estimate the possibility of a plaintiff's verdict as one out of three, or 33.3 percent. But the strength of your case is damages. You estimate the full value of the economic and noneconomic damages at $1 million.

By taking into consideration the liability problems, you arrive at a settlement value that is one-third of the full value of your damages, or in this case, $333,333. This is a realistic number that takes into consideration the problems with liability and damages. Now you've got the settlement value for your case.

The settlement value is the number that sets the absolute floor (aka bottom line) for the settlement negotiations. Under no circumstances will you accept a penny less than the settlement value during the negotiations. Even if the defense lawyers offer $325,000, you will reject the offer.

Okay, but we're just getting started. If all that you had to do was to determine the settlement value, you will not get the great settlements that all plaintiffs' lawyers are working night and day for. So, let's move now to the goal.

How Do Establish the *Goal* for Your Settlement Negotiations

You need to determine a number for the goal of your settlement negotiations. The "goal" is the desired outcome of your negotiation—namely, the best possible outcome that is *realistic*. I italicized *realistic* for a reason: we're still not talking about the full value of your damages. (That number is called the verdict potential, or the potential value of the damages if a jury finds for the plaintiff and awards full damages).

The goal for your settlement negotiations is always higher than the settlement value. But it has to be a realistic number *for a settlement*. The number for the goal is typically 25–30 percent higher than the settlement value.

Let's say you establish that your case has a settlement value of $333,000 (aka bottom line), a realistic number for the goal could be $450,000. Now, you know that you might do better than $450,000 with a jury verdict, but realistically, this is the best number that is possible for a settlement.

Be real with yourself. Of course, I know you could hit big with a seven-figure jury verdict (the potential verdict value), but that's not what we're talking about.

Just because you set the settlement value and the goal at certain numbers *doesn't mean your case won't settle for more*. I often settle cases for more than the goal. You are not limiting the potential settlement by setting realistic numbers for the settlement value and the goal.

How You Can Guarantee That You Don't Settle for Less Than the Settlement Value

Once you have the numbers for the settlement value and the goal, you are ready to have a face-to-face meeting with your client. This is the "get-real" meeting. At this meeting, you sit down with your client to explain how you arrived at the figures from the settlement value and the goal—namely, you explain the weaknesses and strengths of the case.

If you've developed a good rapport with your client before this meeting, your client will usually nod his head in agreement and accept your settlement value and the goal. Once your client has agreed with the numbers, you must get your client to "sign on" to your numbers. Your conversation with the client goes something like this:

> I will never ask you to accept less than the settlement value. You have my word on that. But I want you to give me your word that you will *never agree* to consider a settlement offer that is *less* than the settlement value.

You need to get your clients' solemn vows that they will never accept less than the settlement value even if the final settlement offer is a dollar less than the settlement value. If you leave open the possibility of accepting less than the settlement value, the numbers for your settlement value and the goal are meaningless.

What is the point of setting a settlement value and goal if you don't make a mutual commitment (you and your client) to hold firm with the numbers?

But Be Ready for Temptation (I Promise This Will Happen)

Inevitably, the defense lawyers will make low-ball settlement offers to try to tempt your clients. I call this bait—namely, just enough money to tempt your clients to settle without insulting them. Most injury victims have no money, and even a little money may seem like a lottery award to them.

But your clients aren't the dumb fish that swallow the bait—because they have got you telling them what to do. When the low-ball settlement offer is made, your clients will already be educated on what to do and ready to respond. Your conversation will go something like this:

> We knew the defense lawyer was going to throw a low-ball offer at you to try to settle the case. But the settlement offer was lower than your settlement value, and you gave me your word that you would not accept a penny less than the settlement value. You and I worked hard to establish a settlement value and a goal for the settlement negotiations, and we are going to hold firm to our numbers. So I will reject the settlement offer. Agreed?

During this conversation, your client will reaffirm his commitment to the settlement value and the goal. But your client has to be prepared for this conversation with reinforcement that the settlement value and goal are mutually binding agreements that you will always hold firm to.

But what if your clients balk and want to accept the low-ball settlement offer? You gently remind them: "Do you remember when we met to set the settlement value and the goal for your case? (Of course they do!) During our chat, you agreed that you would not settle for less than $333,000. Are you going back on your word with me?"

Your clients will ultimately agree that you are right and stick with the game plan that was agreed upon with them.

Your Life Just Got a Whole Lot Easier

It's great to have a plan. Once you set a settlement value and a goal for the settlement negotiations, your life just got a whole lot easier. Your authority to settle the case is limited by the numbers agreed upon with your client.

When it comes time for the pretrial settlement conference, you will have a negotiation strategy that is designed to get the top settlement possible (the goal) and you will have a bottom-line number (the settlement value). You know that you cannot settle for less than the settlement value for two reasons: (1) you do not have authority from the client to settle for less than the settlement value, and (2) you gave your word to your client that you will never recommend a settlement that is less than the settlement value.

The pretrial settlement conference just became easy. Either the defense lawyers meet your numbers or they don't. And it's perfectly fine if the settlement offer is less than the settlement value.

If the defense lawyers want to dictate the terms of a settlement, just tell them to go away. If the defense won't be reasonable with their settlement offer, you should hold them to the fire for it. Remember, trial law is what you do and your client hired a "trial lawyer."

The Top Three Mistakes Made with Personal Injury Referrals

This is a common story: A new client, Mr. Jones, comes to your office with a new personal injury case involving an accident in New Jersey. You explain to Mr. Jones that you are not admitted to practice law in the New Jersey, and you refer him to the best personal injury law firm, Dewey, Cheatem and Howe, in New Jersey. You make the connection for Mr. Jones to a New Jersey law firm, and you wish him luck and see him on his way. You don't hear from Mr. Jones for a couple of years. But there's an interesting twist to the story.

Flash forward two years later. You run into Mr. Jones while you're pumping gas, and he thanks you profusely for your referral of Dewey, Cheatem and Howe. Mr. Jones stuns you with his story of how he recovered a high six-figure settlement in his injury case. You exchange pleasantries with Mr. Jones, see him on his way, and you secretly seethe at the discovery that you did not see a single dime from the personal injury settlement.

Once you get over your disgust, you are tempted to call Dewey, Cheatem and Howe to find out why you did not receive a referral fee. After you calm down a bit, you realize that *you have no one to blame but yourself.* You never memorialized the referral of Mr. Jones in writing with Dewey, Cheatem and Howe and in the absence of a written agreement specifying the division of the legal fee, you have no right to any part of the legal fee.

Here are the top three mistakes made by lawyers when referring injury cases:

MISTAKE #1: FAILING TO MEMORIALIZE THE REFERRAL AND THE DIVISION OF THE LEGAL FEE

The biggest mistake that you can make is failing to memorialize the referral in writing on full disclosure to the client. It's really simple: the referral of the client must be memorialized in the retainer agreement (or another document), or you are not entitled to a referral fee. **You must insist that the attorney of record include your name on the retainer agreement that is signed by your client**. The "attorneys of record" are the lawyers handling the lawsuit.

You should also insist that the attorney of record have a separate written agreement with you that specifies the division of the legal fee—namely, the percentage of the legal fee that you will receive at the end of the case. The division of the legal fee between the two law firms must be disclosed to your client under New York's ethical rules.

If your name is not listed on the retainer agreement and you do not have a separate agreement with the attorney of record regarding the division of the legal fee, you will *never recover a penny of the legal fee.* You must protect your rights as the referring lawyer.

You should never agree to a verbal agreement with the attorney of record. Such an agreement is completely unenforceable. If you come to court seeking to enforce a verbal agreement regarding a referral fee, you will be laughed out of court. Don't do this!

Practice tip: Get your name on the retainer agreement and the memorandum concerning the division of the fee at the very beginning when the client first comes to you. Otherwise, you may forget and the attorney of record may hope you don't remember.

MISTAKE #2: FAILING TO INSIST ON A REFERRAL FEE FROM THE ATTORNEY OF RECORD

For some crazy reason, many lawyers do not ask for a referral fee when referring a personal injury case. Why?

Consider this: the attorney of record makes a living by getting referrals of clients from lawyers just like you. The attorney of record can't survive without you and you are ethically permitted to share in the legal fee under New York's ethical rules. So why you are you continuing to refer injury cases without asking for a referral fee?

If you don't ask for a referral fee, the attorney of record will not bring it up. You can't expect most personal injury lawyers to protect your rights to a referral fee. This is your job! You must be proactive in protecting your rights to a referral fee.

Practice tip: When you place the first phone call to another personal injury lawyer, you must start the conversation by saying, "I am referring this client to you on a referral basis. If you accept the referral, my name must be listed on the retainer agreement as the referring attorney, and we must sign a separate agreement specifying the division of the legal fee between our law firms." Once this is confirmed, you should also state the percentage of the legal fee that you will accept: "My referral fee will be one-third of the total fee. If that is not acceptable, I will find another lawyer to take this case." Don't be a wimp!

MISTAKE #3: FAILING TO NEGOTIATE THE DIVISION OF THE LEGAL FEE

Ninety-five percent of referring lawyers agree to the division of the legal fee that is proposed by the attorney of record. In some cases, the "fee split" is non-negotiable, but you can negotiate for a better fee split in many cases.

Let's say you refer a slam-dunk construction accident (Labor Law 240 in personal injury lingo in New York) involving a fall from the roof a commercial property. Your client is severely injured and there is great liability and millions in liability insurance. You call the attorney of record who informs you that your referral fee will be one-third of the total fee. Most lawyers just say, "Thank you" and thank their lucky stars for one-third of the legal fee. Why?

Will it hurt to bargain for a higher percentage of the legal fee? Of course not! The worst that happens is the attorney of record says no. Realize this: *everything is negotiable*, including the division of the legal fee between you and the attorney of record.

Practice tip: In cases with strong liability, substantial injuries, and more than enough insurance coverage, you should bargain for more than the standard one-third referral fee. I've had cases where I've paid 50 percent, and even 75 percent of the legal fee to the referring attorney and I didn't blink. I would not have a penny without the referral so I am always appreciative of the work and have no problems with generous referral fees. You can say to the attorney of record, "I'm willing to accept a 50/50 division of the legal fee. If this is not acceptable, I will speak with other injury lawyers who I am sure will find this acceptable."

Don't hesitate to play hard ball with attorneys of record. You have a mortgage to pay and mouths to feed just as they do.

Part 3
THE ENTREPRENEUR

"For these people who make efforts to limit you and suggest you cannot fulfill your dreams are dangerous people. These people have given up on their dreams and seek to convince you to do the same."

"What they really seek to do is to have you join the ranks of slaves, the apathetic, and the hopeless. Be deaf to them!"

—GRANT CARDONE, *If You're Not First, You're Last*

20

THE WORLD'S BIGGEST HOAX ON LAWYERS

"Every business is really a marketing business."

—John Jantsch, *The Commitment Engine*

YOUR FIRST BIG VERDICT finally comes in! You're on the road to fame and fortune as a trial lawyer … or so you think.

As the great result fades away, you expect a flood of new clients and referrals. But something funny happens. The phone doesn't ring and you're left wondering what happened. You thought that the great outcome would bring you new clients and more money, but that never happens. You're left scratching your head and wondering what you did wrong.

It dawns on you months later that success in the courtroom does not translate into new clients and bigger legal fees. So you go back to doing what you were doing before: taking any case that happens to walk through your door and just hoping that one day you don't have to take the crappy cases.

Who Created This Hoax on Lawyers?

It started the first day you stepped into law school. You walk into the ivy-covered law school with big dreams of courtroom victories, and you learn the basics of contracts, torts, and constitutional law. After three years of law school, you think you're ready to conquer the legal world.

But law school didn't prepare you for the real world.

Once you join a law firm, you discover that success as a lawyer depends a lot more on things that have nothing to do with the rules of evidence, opening statements, or motions in limine. Of course, you have to be able to do those things, but your success depends very little on the technical aspects of taking a lawsuit from beginning to end. Instead, your success hinges on things no one taught you in law school: *having systems for running a law firm, getting new clients, and making money.*

If there's a single inescapable truth I've learned in my career, it's this: *business development is the single most important priority that every lawyer (including you) should have.*

So What Do You Do Now?

Oh, great, you say. No one ever taught you a damn thing about business development, law office systems, or marketing in law school. You convince yourself that it's just fine that you don't venture into this unknown world, and you keep doing what you've always done. Hey, you've got a website and a yellow pages ad, just like every other lawyer, so you think that's enough.

But if you're still reading, there's a good chance you're not happy with the status quo. Let's start with a critical distinction: *you run a business*, not a law firm. Yes, that's right. Contrary to what you've been told by your law professors, lawyer friends, and parents, you are running a business. (BTW: if you want a model for the best business/law firm I've seen in 21 years of practice, you should learn as much as you can about Finkelstein & Partners. They are the gold standard for a business/law firm).

And what is the goal of every business? Yes, that's right (don't be afraid to admit it), your goal is to make as much money as possible. Now, I know what you're thinking: "Fisher is nuts. My goal is to serve my clients and give the best legal representation." Of course it is, but you can't serve your clients if you don't make the payroll. So let's get real about your top priority of making money.

You Must Know Who Your *Ideal Client* Is

First, you must identify your "ideal client." For almost all of us, our ideal client is not the plaintiff or defendant in our cases. So get that thinking out of your head. Our ideal client is the person who brought our client to us in the first place and who continues to bring us a steady stream of new clients.

If you are a real estate lawyer, are your ideal clients the homeowners buying a new home? No! The homeowners will use your services one time for a fee of $750, and you will likely never hear from them again, if ever, until they buy another home in 20 years. You will be broke by the time the homeowners need you again. The ideal clients for the real estate lawyer are the real estate agents who refer a steady stream of new homeowners. Now we're talking.

The goal is *not* to make money on a single transaction. Rather, your goal should be to develop relationships with your ideal client that will generate new clients and a steady stream of income for the rest of your career. The lifetime value of your ideal client is far greater than the value of a single transaction or settlement.

You Must Answer This Question:
Who Is Your Ideal Client?

When cases are resolved, the clients are thrilled, and you think you've got referral sources for the rest of your career. But these clients won't even remember your name in a couple of weeks. And even if the clients happen to remember your name, there's a slim chance they will ever have another case for you. So what's the point of maintaining these relationships?

But your referral partners will remember you, and with the right connection, you may get new referrals every week. As long as you are good at what you do, you will continue getting new cases from your referral partners and once they see your work, they will refer you to their network of lawyers. The spigot has opened and you're in business.

But Once You've Identified Your Ideal Client,
How Do You Create New Relationships
and Nurture Existing Ones?

If you buy a new gardenia and put it in a new planter in your living room, the plant will die if you don't water it at least once a week, right? The same concept applies to your ideal clients: you have to stay in regular contact with them through a variety of ways, including handwritten letters, direct mail newsletters, e-mails to update them on the status of a case, and even tote bags full of bagels.

Why do I write a lawyer newsletter, *Lawyer Alert*, every month? That's right. Because *you* are my ideal client. I cultivate relationships with lawyers through newsletters, trial lawyer workshops, e-mail campaigns, and websites because my ideal client is *you*.

I mail my monthly newsletter at the first of every month so when that next malpractice or catastrophic injury case crosses your desk, you will think of me. (Yes, I have ulterior motives.)

21

YOUR HUGE
COMPETITIVE
ADVANTAGE

ARE YOU A BETTER LAWYER than the guy with the big, bad, double-truck, yellow pages advertisement? You know this guy, the one with a big photo of his face plastered all over buses, billboards, and yellow page ads. (Some of these guys are a little scary looking if you ask me.)

Okay, let's be honest. The lawyer on the big, double-truck advertisements can't hold a candle to your trial skills, knowledge, and case results. You know your stuff and you're willing to go head to head with the big money advertisers. But there's a little problem: you don't have a bank account with a couple of extra million just sitting around to go head to head with the big guns of lawyer advertising.

So, what do you do? Refinance your mortgage and fight back with big, double-truck, yellow page ads? Or perhaps you just concede defeat and go about your business taking any ole' client who walks in the door?

There's an answer, my friend. It's simple and it works—but it takes chutzpah.

Why Lawyer Advertising Sucks!

First, let's start with a basic proposition: *all lawyer advertising sucks!* C'mon, admit it.

It makes no difference whether we're talking about yellow pages ads, TV or radio commercials, or lawyer billboards. They are so bad that we become immune to them. That's right. We don't even notice the obnoxious *"We fight for you"* ads on TV, billboards, and radio. You pick the media—TV, radio, yellow pages or websites—lawyer ads are outrageously bad, distasteful, and obnoxious, and yes, they demean our profession.

If lawyer ads were just ridiculously obnoxious, that would be bad enough. But it's much worse than you can imagine. Here's the critical point: *almost ALL lawyer ads look exactly alike.* You know what I mean: from billboards on major highways with lawyers shouting, "I will fight for you," to TV commercials of lawyers with boxing gloves on. Our profession seems intent on self-destruction.

With lawyer ads that look identical, how would you expect an injury victim to find you? Fat chance, right? Let's face it, you might as well be rolling the dice in a game of craps with the ridiculous lawyer ads that claim, "I will fight for you" or "30 years of combined trial experience." The consumer has no way to work through all the crappy lawyer ads to get to you. This is "random chance marketing" (to coin Bob Battle, Esq.'s phrase)—in other words, just praying the consumer opens the phone book to your yellow pages ad and decides to call you.

THE ANSWER: A LAWYER BILLBOARD THAT STANDS OUT FROM THE CROWD

The answer in two words is: be different! And no, this does not mean, "Free initial consultation," "Weekend appointments available," or "We fight for you." (Do lawyers really fight?)

Okay, great, but how can lawyers create a message to consumers that is unique, cost effective, and makes money? If you live in the

Capital District and drive on Interstate 90 (which is everyone), you have a great example of outside-the-box lawyer advertising that works.

On Interstate 90 in Albany there is a billboard that is unlike any other lawyer advertising you've seen. The billboard of Finkelstein & Partners reads, "Do Not Text and Drive," in plain, bold, red print.

So what's so great about this simple, plain message? Do drivers really put their iPhone down when they read the billboard? Are accidents prevented by this billboard? Who knows? But I can tell you one thing: this billboard is unique in conveying a clear message: *We don't care about getting your next injury case. We care more about your safety.* Brilliant!

Why would a driver take notice of this billboard and ignore the rest? It's simple: the billboard of Finkelstein & Partners conveys a unique message that is different from any you've seen before.

Does this billboard work in getting new clients? It's just a guess on my part, but I've got to imagine it does a hell of a lot better than the standard "We fight for you" lawyer ads that are obnoxious, loud, and depend on pure chance to get new clients. (If I am ruffling a few feathers, too bad.)

HOW YOU CAN STAND OUT FROM THE CROWD OF LAWYER ADVERTISEMENTS

Great, but you don't quite have the budget for a billboard on a major highway? Not a problem, my friend. Here's a tactic that you won't find anyone else doing: educate consumers on how to find the right lawyer for their case.

It's simple: The average injury victim (or bankruptcy or criminal defense client) has no clue how to hire the best lawyer for his case. The consumer is subject to hundreds of lawyer ads every day and has no way to tell who the best lawyer is. So, what do they do? Close their eyes and point to the first yellow pages lawyer ad they find? (Some do, but is that a client you want anyway?)

Instead of the pro forma "30 years of combined trial experience" lawyer ad, you think outside the box. Your ad in the newspaper, website, radio, or TV (the media doesn't matter; the message is what counts) reads, "Discover why 92 percent of injury victims do not recover the full value of their damages" or better yet, "Find out why only one out of eight malpractice victims recover more than a penny." You might offer a free audio CD to injury victims to help them find the right lawyer for their case. What you are really doing is getting injury victims, or prospective clients, to raise their hand for your free stuff and get them to stop their search through the yellow pages.

An excellent young lawyer, John DeGasperis, Esq., once told me that my message is counterintuitive in that I give the answers away. That's right and that's why I do it—*because no one else does*. Other lawyers scream, "We're the greatest lawyers," but the consumer has no way to weed out the good lawyers from the bad.

A LITTLE WARNING: YOU WILL BE MOCKED AND RIDICULED

You will be mocked, laughed at, and ridiculed by your peers with a unique, outside-the-box message. But who cares? Keep in mind these are the same lawyers wearing boxing gloves on lawyer billboards.

And here's a little tip: if you are being laughed at, there's a good chance others are fearful and intimidated by you and want you conform to the status quo just like every other lawyer in your town. The ridicule of your peers is almost always a sign that what you're doing is working.

So take a chance! Throw caution to the wind and you just might be surprised by the results.

Why Lawyer Websites Suck!

The big day finally arrives. Your new whiz-bang website is finally ready to be launched. You've spent a king's ransom on your new website and you're ready for the big payoff. Your new website's got everything: fancy flash animation, award-winning logos, and stories of your big verdicts and settlements. Now you're ready to conquer the Internet world!

But a funny thing happens. Weeks and then months pass after the launching of your new website and you're not getting any new calls or clients. Your webmaster talks you into just giving it a little more time and the money will begin rolling in. But as the months pass, nothing changes: no phone calls and no new clients. Your website isn't doing squat for you.

After a year passes with your high-priced, state-of-the-art website, you demand a face-to-face with your webmaster. Yes, you explain that you love the fancy look of your website, and yes, you love the flash animation and award-winning logos and that your website is on the first page of organic search results with Google, Bing, and Yahoo, but you haven't got a single client from your website. This is when you're told that you just haven't spent enough money on your website and for just another $1,000 bucks a month, all of your problems will be solved.

When you hear those words, *run for the door!*

THE *ONLY* GOAL OF A LAWYER WEBSITE: MAKING MONEY!

Your webmaster will toss around fancy Internet jargon, such as search engine optimization, to throw you off track and convince you to leave everything in her hands. Hey, she's the expert, right? You don't have time to figure out how to build a great lawyer website and you're paying your webmaster big bucks because she's the expert, right?

First, you must keep in mind one very simple premise about lawyer websites: *the single goal of your website is to get new clients and make more money.* Nothing else matters.

Yes, that's right. Having your website found on the first page of the search engines makes absolutely no difference if you're not getting new clients and making money from your website. Having the most gorgeous lawyer website in your county means nothing if you are not getting new cases from the website.

So, the next time you sit down with your webmaster, the conversation should go something like this: "I haven't got a single new case in the last six months from my website. *You're fired!*"

THE BIGGEST MISTAKE MADE ON LAWYER WEBSITES: IT'S NOT ABOUT *YOU*

There's one basic reason why 99 percent of lawyer websites suck: you think your website is about *you*. That's right. You use your website to show off your huge verdicts and settlements and that you have been selected to Super Lawyers for five years straight, and you've written books about your area of practice. Yada, yada, yada. Hell, the consumer would be crazy not to hire you, right?

But that's exactly where 99 percent of lawyers get it wrong. *Consumers don't care about you.* Now, I know your mother and children (and maybe your wife) are impressed by your fancy ivy-league education and your AV rating with Martindale-Hubbell, but no one else gives a crap.

How can you differentiate your practice from the next lawyer down the block when all lawyers are shouting at the top of their lungs the same thing: "I'm the greatest lawyer in the world." The fact is you can't. Consumers have no way to tell the difference between an elite lawyer and a crappy one because lawyer websites have the same content and goal: self-glorification of the lawyer. (Yes, I'm talking about your website!)

So, we start building the website of our dreams with one very simple concept: it's not about you.

HOW TO BUILD THE LAWYER WEBSITE OF YOUR DREAMS

Hey, I know it's tough to get over the concept that lawyer websites are *not* about you. The high-paid sales executives from Findlaw will work long and hard to convince you that you just need to spend more money on your website and the clients will come dancing through your doors. Keep dreaming!

But if you're still reading, there's a good chance you want answers. Okay, what are consumers looking for when they search the Internet for a lawyer? Remember, the consumer has no way to tell a good lawyer from a bad one, so just for the moment, let's forget about your fancy law-school pedigree and your seven-figure settlements and verdicts.

It's really simple: *the consumers want information that helps answer their problem.* Stop and think: what are the ten most frequently asked questions that your clients ask you and what are the ten questions that your clients *should* be asking you. Write these down right now.

Guess what? You just entered the mind of your client. You're writing content for your website that answers the questions that your clients are asking. Instead of browsing the Internet for answers to their problems, consumers will now stop their search once they find a website, like yours, that answers their problems.

But you're just getting started. Every day your clients ask you questions, and you think, "I've been asked that question a million times." Great, write it down. Consumers crave information about deadlines—namely, "How long do I have to sue?" You can write 10–15 frequently asked questions just about the statute of limitations. Now, you're firing on all cylinders.

BUT WHY WOULD YOU GIVE YOUR SECRETS AWAY FOR FREE?

I know what you're thinking: why should I just give away all of the information that it took years to learn (not to mention a boatload of tuition money for law school)? *Because no one else is doing this.* That's right. If you simply do whatever every lawyer on the block is doing, your website will continue to suck.

Earl Nightingale once said, "See what others are doing in your industry and do the opposite."

Nothing could be truer for lawyer websites: *be different* from every other lawyer website in your town. This, more than anything else, is the key to building a dynamic website.

Just think about the best websites that you visit. Stop and write them down right now. I'm willing to bet your list includes WebMD, Ask.com, and Wikipedia, but why? Because these websites are chock-full of great information that you can use.

Now, ponder this question: how many lawyer websites are on your top-10 list of favorite websites? That's right, *none*. That's because lawyer websites suck. But there is no reason your website can't be the WebMD, Ask.com, or Wikipedia (for lawyers).

Yes, Internet marketing works for lawyers and it can work for you. But I'm betting against you; I'm willing to bet that you won't do a damn thing to change your website. Hey, it's up to you to prove me wrong.

Why Mass Marketing Sucks!

It's impossible to ignore.

The loud, obnoxious lawyer advertisements are everywhere. From lawyer billboards to a seemingly endless run of lawyer TV ads, it never seems to end. The consumer is bombarded by mass marketing by lawyers every day and virtually every hour of the day they ignore another pointless lawyer advertisement.

Here's the problem: 99.99% of consumers have no need for your services, so your mass marketing is not focused or directed to a potential client. Consumers just ignore the endless lawyer advertisements on TV, radio and billboards because they have no need for what you're selling.

And just ask yourself: would you hire a lawyer based on a lawyer billboard with a picture of the lawyer saying, "We fight for you"? As New Yorkers say, FUHGEDABOUDIT! And let's face a brutal reality: very few intelligent, rational consumers hire a lawyer based on mass marketing—would you?

WHERE DO YOUR BEST CLIENTS COME FROM?

It's a safe bet that your best clients (those who listen to you and do what you tell them) didn't find you on a lawyer billboard or radio advertisement. Your best clients did not magically show up at your office—they were referred to you. That's right, someone you know told your client to see you.

The relationship with your new client starts with a big smile and handshake that goes like this, "Mr. Jones told me you are the perfect lawyer for my case and I'd love for you to take my case." Somehow (almost magically) you just met a total stranger who has complete trust and confidence in you.

WHAT BERNIE MADOFF CAN TEACH ALL OF US

All of the goodwill that your referral partner has built with the new client is transferred to you (remember Bernie Madoff—though he was a criminal, he was a master at referral marketing). Just think how Madoff got started: all it took was a single referral from a prominent business person in NYC and with the transfer of trust from just a single referral source, some of the biggest non-profit organizations in the northeast were begging Madoff to handle their investments.

The lesson from Bernie Madoff: if you earn the trust and confidence of a single referral partner, your partner will refer you to others within her sphere of influence and suddenly, the floodgates open with new referrals. It all starts with a single relationship with a powerful and influential person.

YOU WILL NEVER MAKE A MISTAKE AGAIN

Even if you make mistakes (we all do), your client is understanding, forgives your oversights and just feels lucky you are her lawyer. You are a virtual god to your new client from day one and it stays that way throughout the lawsuit. You would have to mess up big time to screw this up.

But it gets even better: your referral partner has evaluated the case for merit, obtained and prepackaged the medical records and maybe sent you a case summary evaluating the strengths and weaknesses of the case. You're handed a great new case on a silver platter and your new client loves you before you even meet. Hell, it doesn't get much better than this!

HOW TO GET THE BEST RETURN ON INVESTMENT FOR YOUR MONEY

You know your "A" cases come from referrals and the cases that you get from mass marketing are absolute junk (yes, there are exceptions, but stick with me). So, then, why do all lawyers focus their time and money on mass marketing? Is your money really spent wisely on yellow page ads, TV and radio ads and billboards? I'm willing to bet you have no idea what return on investment you get from mass marketing.

But you know that the return on investment ("ROI") that you get from referrals blows away any mass marketing that you do. Okay, so why do lawyers have huge budgets and grandiose marketing plans for mass marketing, but absolutely no plan for referral marketing? This is truly nutty.

A MINDSET REVOLUTION FOR YOU

What if you decided to begin thinking of referral marketing as the highest and best use of your marketing dollar? Okay, sounds great, you say, but how the hell do you market to your top referral partners? Guess what, I'm doing it RIGHT NOW. That's right, YOU are my top referral partners. I mail my monthly newsletter, Lawyer Alert, to you on the twenty-sixth day of every month to stay "top of mind" with my top referral partners (I know, it's sneaky). And the costs of this newsletter are minuscule compared to the referrals and the fees from your referrals. Talk about return on investment: there is no higher return on investment than a monthly newsletter sent to your best referral partners (a/k/a your "Ideal Client").

But lawyers just want to conform and do what everyone else is doing. Hell, we're all afraid of what others will think of us and we conform our actions to what we think will be accepted and approved by our peers. **This is the biggest mistake you can make.**

IDENTIFYING YOUR IDEAL CLIENT

You begin by identifying the top 5 referral partners you have—write them down right now. And no, it's not just a numbers game—think of the lawyer or non-lawyer who sends the highest quality cases to you, e.g., the cases that make the most money for you. The best cases that make you feel great you're a lawyer and pay your bills. Guess what, you just identified your Ideal Client!

Once you know who your top 5 Ideal Clients are, you create a systematic plan for staying top of mind with them through a monthly newsletter, weekly emails, CLE seminars and workshops, tote bags full of bagels, handwritten notes on personal stationary, complimentary cocktail hours, lunch dates, and just about anything you can think of.

It really doesn't matter what you do—just that you do SOMETHING and have a game plan in place for regularly reaching out to your top referral partners. But as crazy as it seems, most lawyers do absolutely nothing to stay top of mind with their referral partners and just keep spending their hard-earned cash on the mass marketing vultures.

SAY GOODBYE TO MASS MARKETING...FOREVER

You think outside the box with a novel, unique marketing plan that is targeted to your Ideal Clients who know and trust you. Unlike any of your peers, you create a plan to cultivate and nurture your Ideal Clients who will refer a steady stream of new cases to you for the rest of your career...and you can say goodbye to the mass marketing vultures.

THE HUGE MISTAKE THAT ALL LAWYERS MAKE (and what you can do to avoid it)

You know you should expect it, but every time it happens, you're just as surprised.

When you get a tremendous settlement or verdict in a big case, your client wants to adopt you as a new member of their family. It's not just a handshake and smiles—it's hugs and kisses with your client when their case ends. You've built a strong and lasting relationship with your client over the course of the lawsuit and love is in the air. After all of the details of the case are finalized, you part ways with your client certain of one thing: you will be their hero for life.

Not so fast, my friend. Fast forward a couple of months to when your client is asked about the outcome of their lawsuit at a party. Your client is effusive with praise for your work and the outcome, "My lawyer was amazing," but then a funny thing happens. When asked for your name, your client looks up in the air, pauses, thinks hard for 15 seconds, shakes his head and then throws up his hands and just mumbles, "I'll think of his name—give me some time." That's right, *your client can't even remember your name!*

Now, I know what you're thinking. This would never happen to you. You are a god to your clients—they love you to death and you will have a place permanently etched in their hearts and minds. And, of course they would, you changed their life with an amazing settlement or verdict. You think, "How could they ever forget me?"

A HARSH REALITY THAT YOU MUST FACE

But you're kidding yourself! Once their case is over, your clients will forget you and most will not even remember your name. Your client is no longer a source for referring new clients to you.

So, you feel a little betrayed and think that maybe you just weren't as important to your clients as you thought. But that's not true. It's just your clients have lives too and once their case is over, they move on to the business of getting on with their life and they quickly put their lawsuit behind them somewhere deep in the vault of their memory.

But here's the problem: *if your clients can't even remember your name, they will never refer new clients to you.* This is a MAJOR PROBLEM. One of your top referral sources can't even remember your name and you will get no future clients from a client you thought was a raving fan.

FIRST, THE PROBLEM: YOU

Lawyers want the quick buck, the easy kill and in the world of personal injury, this means the injury victim who just got run over by a tractor trailer and is in the intensive care unit of the local hospital. You see dollar signs the moment you get the call to go visit the client in the hospital. You think, "If only I could get more cases like this."

You want to make a quick buck whenever you spend a penny on advertising. How do you get the phone to ring so you get the next multi-million dollar case? All lawyers make the same mistake by thinking about the immediate and overlooking the future.

> *"Nothing is about today. Everything is about tomorrow."*
>
> —John Morgan, Esq., *You Can't Teach Hungry*

Instead of planting, cultivating and harvesting, you want to plant and harvest right away. You spend $10 and want $100 back NOW. You have no patience—like all the suckers playing the lottery and pinning their future on a fantasy, you want the quick hit, the big buck with an easy and fast payday. But building the perfect law firm takes time and although it's hard to admit, there are no quick fixes.

HOW TO CULTIVATE YOUR GARDEN

But what can you do to cultivate your garden and think long-term by nurturing your fan base and top referral partners? First, you must have a single goal: to stay TOP OF MIND with your present and former clients, referral partners (a.k.a. lawyers who refer new clients to you), members of the media and friends and prominent business owners who can send new work to you.

Easier said than done, right? Let's face one hard, cold fact: it will be impossible for you to stay "top of mind" with your referral sources with your busy workday. You've got depositions, trials, conferences and paperwork to get done. So, do you just give up and hope the phone rings with your next big case?

There's a solution—it's simple, pretty easy to do and can be automated with little effort on your part. A marketing automation plan ("MAP") will automate the process of keeping you in virtual constant contact with your raving fan base. It's simple, you schedule a sequence of follow-up events that might consist of birthday and anniversary cards, informative and educational emails, voice broadcast, direct mail and e-mail newsletters and text messages and voila! You're staying top of mind with your top referral sources weekly, monthly or as often as you want.

You sit back and watch the cases come through your front door. But even better, your clients call you to thank you for the anniversary card and your thoughtful reminders and safety tips. You've just automated the growth of your law firm and your automated follow up system doesn't rely on you to do a damn thing. You could be sitting on a beach in Cancun while your automated marketing machine is doing its thing. How beautiful is that?

With a marketing automation plan in place, you're no longer just planting the seeds and harvesting right away. Now, you're planting, CULTIVATING and slowly but surely harvesting the fruits of your dynamic growth engine. You're planning for the future instead of doing what all other lawyers do, looking for the quick and easy buck.

THE BEST MARKETING GROWTH ENGINE ON THE PLANET

But there's one little problem—no one does it! No other lawyer you know is doing this so it must be a stupid idea, right? But take a look around you—the majority of lawyers are desperate for new cases and just fighting for any scraps they can get. If you do what every other lawyer in your town is doing, you'll be faced with a career of crappy cases that will just barely pay your bills.

Here's the answer for you: Infusionsoft. Yes, there are other companies that automate email response, like AWeber or Constant Contact, but don't waste your time. Infusionsoft is an amazing software company (Goldman Sacs recently invested $54 million in this small, mom and pop business in Arizona) that will do everything for you—not just e-mail, but faxes, text messages, voice broadcast and direct mail and postcards. You get everything under one roof.

And here's the beauty of it for you: once you schedule your automated follow up sequences in Infusionsoft with a program called the Campaign Builder, your work is done. You can sit back, let the marketing automation plan do its work and now, you're staying top of mind with your raving fan base. Your life just got a whole lot easier, right?

But don't kid yourself into thinking you can set up a complex marketing automation plan. Let the experts at Infusionsoft, or their outside consultants, set up the systems for automating your follow up with your fan base and let the magic of automation do its thing.

WHY YOU WON'T DO A DAMN THING

I know what you're thinking, "Why would I go to all of that trouble when this client doesn't have a case with me anymore?" But this is exactly where you're selling yourself short by focusing on the quick and easy dollar and not thinking about tomorrow.

> *"Most of the world vehemently refuses to spend time on actions that won't immediately pay off."*
>
> —GRANT CARDONE, *If You're Not First, You're Last*

Every person you know has a sphere of influence consisting of roughly 50 family and friends—these are people who your clients speak to just above every week to make recommendations about clothing, restaurants and yes, lawyers. Even if your client doesn't have a new case for you today, there's a good chance he'll have a case to refer to you six months from now. And even if your client never has a new case of his own, there's a decent chance he'll refer his ex-girlfriend or an old buddy from high school—the possibilities that someone from within your client's sphere of influence will have a new case for you are way too strong to ignore.

But unless you stay top of mind with your former clients and top referral sources, you will never tap into the power of your raving fan base. You'll remain the one trick pony looking for the quick cash like every other lawyer in your town.

But don't take my word for it. Discover for yourself why Goldman Sacs invested $54 million in Infusionsoft and you will be on your way to unlocking the secret to planting, cultivating and harvesting the power of your raving fan base for the long-term growth of your law practice.

22

HOW YOUR WEBSITE CAN BECOME A POWERFUL CLIENT MAGNET

FIRST, YOU NEED A WEBSITE to which you can add new content—for example, web pages—as often as you want at no extra cost. If your webmaster charges you for adding new web pages, fire him now!

More than anything else, the success of your website will be determined by how much new content you add to the website every single day. *Content is king.* If you ignore your website, it will ignore you.

While there are many webmasters competing for your business, there are just a few who grasp the only two concepts you need to know:

1. You must have the ability to add new web pages to your website whenever, and as often as you want.

2. It's not about *you*.

The goal of Internet marketing is to provide valuable, free information that consumers will crave. Don't pitch consumers with your big courtroom victories. Instead, "Wow!" them with information about the mistakes you've made and how you've learned from your mistakes. Consumers will love you for this.

Webmasters will get techy on you by pitching you with fancy technical jargon that you've never heard of. Don't listen to this nonsense. If you follow the two concepts of adding new content to your website every day and providing valuable information that consumers want, you will be on your way to building an asset for your law practice.

As you get busy building your information powerhouse website, you will be amazed at the new cases you get from all over the country and, in fact, the world. You can begin referring cases to trial lawyers outside your state and getting big referral fees just for making the referral. It doesn't get much better than that.

The Three Biggest Mistakes Made on Lawyer Websites

Have you ever noticed that every lawyer website looks the same? And it's not just the images of Lady Liberty or the city skyline on the home page. Lawyer websites all look alike, and for you, that is a huge competitive advantage—if you build a website that is unlike any other lawyer website.

But what are the key essentials to a killer website that almost all lawyer websites lack?

MISTAKE #1: THE ABSENCE OF A "CALL TO ACTION"

Most lawyer websites don't have a "call to action." And no, your phone number or a new client contact form is not a "call to action." This is the number-one mistake made by lawyer websites.

A "call to action" gives the consumers a compelling offer that almost forces them to stop browsing the Internet and call you with their new case. Think late-night TV infomercials: "If you're one of the first 15 callers, you'll get bonus Ginsu knives—but only for the next five minutes." That's great stuff—you almost have to stop what you're doing and buy the Ginsu knives immediately or you'll lose out on this incredible offer. Now use this concept with your website.

The best call to action on a lawyer website belongs to Ben Glass, Esq. The home page (and just about every page of Ben's website) has a big warning: "Before you speak to the insurance adjuster or sign any forms, get my FREE book." You'd have to be crazy to call the insurance adjuster before getting Ben's free book. Why would you keep browsing lawyer websites when Ben Glass, Esq. is offering a free book?

There is no better call to action than a free book. But let's say you don't have time to write a book. You can offer a three-page special report, or a five-minute audio CD recorded on your son's iTouch. It really doesn't matter what you choose as your call to action, but you've got to have something and preferably multiple calls to action on every web page.

You will have a huge competitive advantage over your peers if you only add a single call to action to your website. Trust me. No other lawyers are doing this.

MISTAKE #2: THE FAILURE TO ADD NEW CONTENT *DAILY* TO THE WEBSITE

Lawyers screw this up more than anything else. It's not enough to have a website and just leave it alone. You will get no new clients with a brochure website or a static website. Brochure websites suck!

But I know what you're thinking: I don't have enough time in the day to handle my caseload; how the hell am I going to add new content daily to my website? Good question. You're not going to add new content to your website; you're going to hire someone to do that for you.

For several years now, I've had law review students at the local law school writing content for my website, and guess what? That law student does a better job than you or I could do. For a little over $100 a week, the law student will write fantastic content of cutting-edge legal issues in your community, and before long, you're rocking the Internet!

Whether you hire a law student or pay a content writing company such as We Do Content, you've got to have a plan to add new content to your website *daily*. If you're not adding new content to your website daily, you are wasting your money with internet marketing.

MISTAKE #3: THE LACK OF A FOLLOW-UP CAMPAIGN (AKA "BACK END")

Let's say you're finally rocking the Internet with new leads and contacts from your website. But you now have a new problem: what do you do with all of these new leads? This is a problem very few lawyers even bother to think about. *The lack of follow-up is the number-one mistake in all marketing.* Not just lawyers; all businesses fail to follow up and nurture new leads.

But there's a solution and it's damn good: you need an automated follow-up campaign for new leads and contacts generated by your website. When a new client asks for your free book or special report through your website's multiple calls to action, you need a way to automatically and quickly fulfill the request. The requests for your free materials can be fulfilled automatically by e-mail or direct mail.

E-mail autoresponders: E-mail autoresponders automatically fulfill requests for your free offers by e-mail. The consumers get an instant response to their request. But that's just where you're getting started.

After the initial request is fulfilled through an autoresponder, you should follow up with a sequence of e-mails in order to stay top of mind with your prospective client. Perhaps your second e-mail seeks confirmation that your prospective client received the free materials (book or special report) and your subsequent e-mails provide new information that is relevant to the initial request made by the consumer.

Now you're doing business in your sleep. While you're sleeping, your autoresponders are fulfilling requests for information and following up with new leads on an automatic schedule that you set in advance. Most of your prospective clients don't know that you're sleeping. Many think you are writing e-mails in real time. This is the beauty of an automated sequence of e-mails that keeps you top of mind with your clients.

Direct mail fulfillment: But e-mail is not enough. Most e-mails are opened by less than 15 percent of people due to spam filters or just general indifference to e-mail. You can't rely only on e-mail for the fulfillment of requests for your free offers.

The number-one way to fulfill requests for free information is direct mail. It has always been that way, and it always will. *Direct mail is marketing gold.*

Link Building Secrets for Lawyers

When popular websites have links to your lawyer website, the search engines (Google, Bing, and Yahoo) will give your website a higher ranking on the organic search results—namely, you will show up on page one of a Google search. It's important to have links to your website from other prominent websites. But how do you get links to your website?

It's not nearly as hard as the webmasters make it sound. You have vendors with whom you do business almost every day—perhaps they are a videographer, court-room exhibit expert, stenographer, civil case management software company, and so on. The list of people who make money from you is long. Your vendors are eager to make you happy, and guess what? Your vendors have websites and most will be willing to give your website a link from their website.

It's too easy to simply ask your vendors for a link. Instead, give your vendors something of value by offering a review/testimonial about their services that they can put on their website—for example, "Joe Stenographer is the greatest." You write the testimonial with a link back to your website and ask your vendor to put the testimonial on their website. Roughly 80 percent of the time your vendors will agree.

You're building good will with your vendors and they are giving you high-quality links back to your website. It's a win-win. But almost no one does this. Instead, most lawyers hire expensive Internet "experts" to create link-building campaigns because they don't have enough time to do it themselves. While this is better than doing nothing, the more effective link-building campaign is to get links from your vendors.

Warning! You never want to buy links from websites. This is "black-hat SEO" and the search engines will blacklist your website if you're caught buying links. Don't do it!

How to Build Your Internet Presence with Lawyer Registries

There are a number of great lawyer websites where you can register your profile and get a link to your website. These are websites with high rankings with Google that will give you a link back to your website and thus move your website up in the organic search rankings. Some of the top lawyer registries are www.nolo.com, www.hg.org, www.cornell.edu, and www.lawyers.com, but there is an abundance of lawyer registries on the market.

The lawyer registries cost a little money and they will not drive new clients to you. While you will not get new clients from lawyer registries, they will help you build an Internet presence that will help you dominate the first page of the search engines. Each lawyer registry gives you one more spot on the first page of the search results and thus puts your competitors lower on the search results and maybe even off the first page of Google.

Local Listings with Google, Yahoo, and Bing

Before you do anything else, make sure you grab your local listing with Google, Yahoo, and Bing. The "local listing" (Google Local, Yahoo Local, and Bing Local) are the listings for your business that appear "above the scroll" on Internet searches with a map of your law office location. You can create a profile for your law firm at www. google.com/local, www.local.yahoo.com, and www.bing.com/local. It's easy to do and it's free.

Why You Must Have a Mobile Website

More people use mobile phones rather than PCs to get online. Yes, more consumers are searching for your law firm on a smart phone than on a personal computer. What does this mean for you?

Every page on your website must be converted into a mobile website. A "mobile website" just means that the pages on your website can be read easily with a smart phone. If you don't get a mobile website, your website will appear on a mobile phone in tiny print that is illegible. A mobile website adapts the size of your web pages to the screen of the mobile phone, and thus, makes your website easy to navigate and read for mobile phones.

Most webmasters will offer a free mobile website, but don't assume your webmaster is automatically giving you a mobile website. In most cases, you have to ask. But don't stop there. Get Google

Analytics for your mobile website that shows the number of mobile searches of your website, the number of page views on mobile phones, and the number of persons who contacted you using a mobile phone.

How to Tell if Your Website Is Working

The best *free* tool to find out whether your website is working is Google Analytics. Do you want to know how many people visited your website last week? It's easy. Google Analytics will tell you how many people visited your website, how long the average visitor stayed on your website (the "bounce rate"), and the most popular web pages on your website. You can track the results daily, weekly, monthly, yearly, or however you wish.

You can get Google Analytics for free just by creating a profile with Google.

23

CRAZY, OUTSIDE-THE-BOX MARKETING FOR LAWYERS THAT ACTUALLY WORKS

EVERY LAWYER (hell, every consumer) dreams of quick, easy money. And to get the easy money, lawyers salivate over the next shiny new object in marketing, whether that is a big billboard on a highway with lawyers wearing boxing gloves promising "we'll fight for you," double-truck yellow pages ads that look identical to every other ad, or a loud obnoxious TV commercial with lawyers pretending to be baseball players hitting a home run.

Let's face it, the sales guy couldn't ask for an easier job. It doesn't take much time before the injury lawyers are pulling out their credit cards and charging loads of cash for the "next big thing" that they're convinced will make them rich. Before long, all of the lawyers in town want a cut of the action.

Mass Marketing Is Fool's Gold—At Least for Us

Now don't get me wrong. Mass marketing works just fine for law firms with a $3 million marketing budget that can out-spend every other lawyer in their market. The mass marketers invest a fortune to get every injury victim to call them. And let's face the truth: This type of mass marketing works very well for them. The mass marketers have thousands of cases and have former insurance adjusters settling cases around the clock. Thousands of cases and hundreds of small settlements are the backbone of the mass marketers.

But let's face a cold reality: you can't compete with the mass marketers (and neither can I). Even if you had a couple of million bucks, you have other plans for your cash such as paying for your kids' college tuition. So what do you do? Give up?

Well, as a matter of fact, yes. Don't bother competing against the mass marketers. Instead, you forge a unique path unlike any other lawyer you know. You have a unique, outside-the-box marketing plan that is copied by no one and leaves your peers scratching their heads and cursing you.

Your World Will Change with a Mindset Transformation

Ninety-nine percent of lawyers try to out-yell their competition. The brash claims in lawyer advertising are beyond ridiculous, and injury victims have no way to determine that you are, in fact, better than the next guy on the billboard down the highway. You are fighting a losing battle and the sales guys are just licking their chops.

> *"I was smart enough to understand that just copying what other lawyers were doing with their marketing would be a foolproof recipe for financial ruin."*
>
> —BEN GLASS, ESQ., *Great Legal Marketing*

But what would happen if you stopped yelling "I'm the greatest lawyer"? This may be alien to you, but just stay with me for a minute. Let's stop competing with the masses, who will always drown out our message. Instead, let's try a whole different kind of message, *a message that has nothing to do with you.*

I know it's not easy. Years and years of indoctrination have led you down only one path: that you have to scream, "I'm the best lawyer in the world" and just pray that a consumer believes you. But you need a massive mindset overhaul.

It Starts with a Simple Concept

You have to accept one basic principle: *it's not about you.* That's right. The consumers don't care about you. The consumers want to know what you can do to help them. That's it. Nothing else matters. The consumers don't care that you drive a Mercedes-Benz or wear a $1,000 suit. Those artifacts have always been pointless.

The consumer has questions and you want to answer them, all of them, and in as much detail as you can through as many different forms of media as possible. *You want to become an information powerhouse.* Every day you slowly but surely build an asset by answering more questions, and you don't stop. Your pyramid (aka your law practice) is getting built one brick at a time.

But where do you start first? Blogs, websites, advertisements in radio or TV? There are just about a million different forms of media, and guess what? None of them are bad. *The message is what counts.*

You have to start somewhere, and you've got limited funds to start building your assets. So let's start where you can get the biggest bang for your buck.

But First, a Confession from Yours Truly

I fail 97 percent of the time. That's right. I have a horrible success record when it comes to marketing. I am a miserable failure, and I spend a lot of cash on marketing projects that don't work—but not always. And when I finally find a marketing media or message that works—Yahtsee! (I don't even know what "Yahtsee!" means.)

> *"Every failure brings with it the seed of an equivalent success."*
>
> —Napoleon Hill, *Think & Grow Rich*

Through trial and error with different messages and media, I've found three basic forms of marketing that rule over all others. If I had to choose between only three forms of media for marketing a law practice, it would be a no-brainer: website, newsletters, and event marketing (in no particular order since they're all powerful).

Three Simple Marketing Tools That Will Make All the Difference

Three simple pieces of a unique and dynamic marketing machine:

1. An Information-powerhouse website that provides killer content on a daily basis;

2. A *monthly* newsletter targeted to your ideal client;

3. Regular seminars and workshops that provide valuable content to your ideal client.

It's that simple. If you do nothing else, you're still ahead of 98 percent of all of the lawyers in your town. Yes, it's simple, but it's also simple not to do.

Newsletters

MONTHLY NEWSLETTERS ARE MARKETING GOLD

I know what you're thinking. All of the newsletters you get from lawyers are absolute crap. And you're right; they are. All of us receive generic newsletters, usually from elder law attorneys, that have generic information you can just tell was created by some big national company and formatted to add the lawyer's logo and photograph.

Generic newsletters are easy to send and reasonably affordable, but they are junk. You instantly know what you're getting: a mass mailing with little valuable information. And you toss the newsletter into the trash. The generic newsletter is not what we're talking about.

You shouldn't do a newsletter unless you write the newsletter. The newsletter must have your personality in it, or your targeted clients will know they're just getting another mass mailing. Yes, it takes two hours a month to write a newsletter. But once you've written the copy for the newsletter, the rest is easy: you e-mail the copy to your graphic designer and it's done. Your graphic designer formats the newsletter, adds graphics, and then sends the newsletter to your ful-fillment provider for printing and mailing. It's really not hard at all.

THE NUMBER-ONE REASON WHY NEWSLETTERS FAIL

Most lawyers start with a newsletter by dipping their feet in the water with a quarterly newsletter or bimonthly. *Don't bother wasting your time!* A big secret to newsletters is that they must be mailed monthly. If you don't have two hours a month to write a newsletter, marketing and the growth of your law firm is not a priority for you (though, of course, it should be).

Lawyers don't do newsletters, at least not the kind we're talking about, and it is a huge mistake. *There is no higher return on investment of any form of marketing than newsletters.* Lawyers are lazy and are always looking for the easy way to do things. But once you get a system in place for a monthly newsletter, it will only take two hours out of your month to have a unique newsletter that puts the generic newsletters to shame. That's it: two hours.

So how do you get this done with your busy trial calendar? You need a plan: Block out two hours every month, preferably the same time and day of the month—for example, 8:00 p.m. to 10:00 p.m. on the eighteenth of every month. You will commit to writing the copy for the newsletter at the same time and on the same day every month. But here's the catch: you must treat those two hours the same as you would a court appointment. Those two hours are committed to writing copy for the newsletter and nothing else.

HOW TO WRITE GREAT CONTENT FOR NEWSLETTERS

What do you write about? You should always be thinking of, and on the watch for, content for your newsletter, so by the time you sit down to write the newsletter, you've got an outline of three or four articles. Keep a journal of the ideas for articles that pop into your mind throughout the month. When it comes time to write the newsletter, you'll have much more content than you can fit into the newsletter.

I write a main article on the first and second pages, and on the third and fourth pages, I add a question and answer about a legal topic, one or two testimonials from clients or referral partners ("What They're Saying"), an article about recent settlements ("From John's Casebook"), and an article about different events I'm doing ("What Is John Up To?"). I throw in a couple of goofy photographs of my kids and voilà! The newsletter is done. Adding a personal touch to your newsletter—such as photos of your kids—is a great way to humanize you with your readers.

But here's the secret: your newsletter content must be valuable to your readers, so valuable that they keep all of your newsletters and post them on a bulletin board in the reception area of their office. This is the "multiplicity effect": having your newsletter seen in law firms throughout your community and staying top of mind with your referral partners even when you're on vacation in the Caribbean. While you're sitting on a beach, dozens or hundreds of your referral partners are reading your newsletter or seeing your newsletter on the bulletin board in their reception area. (Yes, this actually happens.)

WHY IS A MONTHLY NEWSLETTER MARKETING GOLD?

It's really simple: because no one has a newsletter! That's right. I'm not counting the generic junk newsletters that you toss in the garbage. We're talking about unique, customized newsletters that grab your audience's attention and provide such great content that your referral partners keep all of your newsletters.

It's so easy to do but also easy not to do (as author Jeff Olsen says in his book *The Slight Edge*). *There is no marketing I've done in my career that has provided a higher return on investment than a monthly newsletter.* I get two to three new case referrals every time I mail my newsletter, and I use it to promote seminars, workshops, podcasts, and new books. Monthly newsletters are a dynamic marketing growth engine.

Just with a monthly newsletter alone (and nothing else), you will be so far ahead of your competition it's crazy. But don't just try one or two newsletters. This won't work. Send newsletters every month for one year, and at the end of that year, you'll be kicking yourself for not doing this earlier in your career.

Event Marketing

Warning! Event marketing is not for the faint of heart. But event marketing, consisting of lawyer workshops and seminars, is easily the most fun you can have in marketing and an exceptional lead generating tool.

I have two trial lawyer workshops, "How to Read the Mind of the Jurors in Your Next Trial" (aka "The Jury Project") and "How to Get Your Law Firm's Website on the First Page of Google ... and Three Things Your Webmaster Won't Tell You." The lawyer workshops are educational, informative, and fun. I offer free written materials and audio CDs that give away all of the secrets about focus groups and internet marketing.

But why give the secrets away for free? You've guessed it by now: because no one else is doing this. To succeed as a lawyer/entrepreneur, you must be *different* from your peers.

BUT WHAT'S THE POINT OF A *FREE* LAWYER WORKSHOP?

Before you get started, you identify your ideal client. For real estate lawyers, your ideal client might be real estate brokers who can send you a steady stream of clients over the course of your career. You should write a list of the top 20 realtors you want to attend your seminar and then promote the hell out of your event with your targets.

You've got your list of the top 20 "targets," or your ideal clients. Now what do you do? You begin by mailing an invitation to your ideal clients and then follow up with a sequence of postcards, e-mails, and even handwritten notes. (Hey, no one said it's easy.)

In all of your promotional materials, you should provide testimonials from others who attended the event. Keep building the momentum for your workshop every day with announcements in your county's bar association and word of mouth everywhere you go. You must set a deadline for your "targets" to RSVP.

WHAT IF NO ONE ATTENDS YOUR WORKSHOP?

Here's a little secret that no one will tell you: If you get a very poor response to your promotion of the workshop, you have to get aggressive. Yes, this means going door to door to the top 5–10 persons whom you want to attend. Bring promotional materials and chocolates. Believe me, this works, and the response rate will go up just with a few office visits.

But even better, contact the county bar association to ask that it promotes your event as a continuing legal education. County bar associations are always looking for new events for their members and if you get them to sponsor your event, your costs just went way down.

Another tip for the savvy: get a sponsor for your workshop to pay the expenses. You have vendors, perhaps a videographer or stenographer, who would love to get a free endorsement of their business at your workshop. And here's the deal: in exchange for providing their services at your workshop, the vendors will get a strong endorsement at the event.

Your vendors will love the free plugs you give them and after a few workshops, your vendors will be fighting to be the sponsor for your workshop. So, you have a great event that puts you in front of your ideal clients; you limit the expenses through having a sponsor; and the county bar association promotes the event among its members. Now you're rocking!

THE KEY TO A SUCCESSFUL WORKSHOP: FOLLOW-UP

But it's not just about having fun and meeting new referral partners. Event marketing is worth its weight in gold only if you do this one thing: *follow up*. When your referral partners arrive at your workshop, you must get their names, addresses, and e-mails, and when the workshop is over, your work is just beginning.

You follow up with a handwritten thank-you note, and perhaps send a special report or a copy of your book. But you're just getting started. Every attendee must be added to your mailing list for your monthly newsletter. If 34 persons attended your workshop, you just added 34 new referral partners—if you follow up with them.

Workshops are crazy fun and pay off in a big way. It takes a little courage to show up and teach lawyers older than you, but once you've done one, it's a piece of cake. I'm willing to bet that (apart from a few elder law attorneys) there is no lawyer in your community who does *any* event marketing. And that's precisely why you should.

Even if you can't get a sponsor to pay for the costs, the return on investment for event marketing is much higher than any other marketing you can do with the only exception being newsletters.

Extra Marketing Gems

Let's say you're on a real tight budget and you can't borrow money from your girlfriend to start a newsletter, website, or put on a workshop. You're more concerned about just paying the rent this month. No problem, my friend.

GRASSROOTS MARKETING AT ITS BEST

If you can scratch together $50, go to your local bagel or donut shop and buy six dozen bagels or doughnuts. Put the goodies in a tote bag and bring them to the offices of your ideal clients with a handwritten note. But don't stop there. Ask to speak with your ideal client when you hand deliver the breakfast for the firm.

The staff will love you for this, but it might not work at first. You will have to be persistent. Go back next Friday with the same tote bag full of bagels, and you might have to do it again. But eventually, you will get the attention of your ideal client, and when that happens, you just got a referral partner who will last the rest of your career.

HANDWRITTEN NOTES ON STATIONARY SHOULD BE A DAILY PRACTICE

Okay, so you don't have $50 for the bagels? No problem. Every day (not every week or month) you should write a handwritten note to your ideal clients. What do you say? Anything. What you say is not important. What is important is that you are staying top of mind with your referral partners so one day when they have business to refer, they will think of you.

But here's a little tip if you want to be clever: Read your local newspaper to find out who was just promoted to partner or won a big verdict. Then, cut out the newspaper story, laminate it, and send the laminated copy of the story to your referral partner with a handwritten note. Very cool! You just won the heart of a referral partner for pennies. And guess what? Your referral partners will always keep those laminated newspaper stories, which will remind them of you.

THERE'S NOTHING LIKE A PARTY

If you really want to get crazy, throw a party for your referral partners. There is nothing better than meeting your referral partners in a social setting and having a few cocktails among friends. It doesn't have to be anything fancy—maybe a happy hour in the popular hangout near the courthouse. A party is just another chance to be different from your peers … and it's a lot of fun.

GET OTHERS TO SAY HOW GREAT YOU ARE WITH TESTIMONIALS

Testimonials are *gold*. Rather than shouting to the world that you are the "greatest lawyer," it's a hundred times more effective and credible to have others say how great you are. Consumers trust testimonials, but they don't trust you.

Why do so few lawyers use testimonials? You should get in the mindset of asking for testimonials every day. Whenever clients or referral partners thank you for something, you should send them an e-mail or ask them in person for a testimonial. The worst that happens is they won't do it—big deal! You will be surprised how many clients and referral partners want to give you a testimonial.

By asking for testimonials on a daily basis, you will build a bank of testimonials that you can use as a promotional item for prospective clients. When a new client is "lawyer shopping" a new case, you can e-mail the testimonials that you've received from your website, www.avvo.com, or Google Local. *No other lawyer is doing this.*

Video testimonials are the best, but even if you can only get a text testimonial, you're way ahead of your competition. Testimonial Director is a great website (www.testimonialdirector.com) for building testimonials and teaching you how to use testimonials for your law practice.

Little tip: get testimonials from your adversaries—for example, the defense lawyers with whom you've had battles. A testimonial from your adversary is the best evidence of your abilities and consumers and referral partners will love them.

The Greatest Business Card you will ever have

Just think, when is the last time you held on to a business card that you got from another lawyer? Sure, maybe you kept the business card in your wallet for a couple of days just 'cause you felt guilty tossing it out right away. But 99% of the time, you toss the business cards into the garbage and never give them another thought.

Let's start with one basic fact: business cards are pretty much a waste of paper. You hand them out at depositions and bar association dinners, but garbage pales are littered with business cards at the courthouse and restaurants. But conventional lawyer wisdom tells you that handing out a ton of business cards will be good for business—NONSENSE!

But what if you had a business card that was indestructible? What if you had a business card that was so good that no one EVER threw it into the garbage? This is the dream come true of all business cards—you stay present in the minds of your clients with the business card of your dreams. You have a business card unlike any other lawyer and you violate all industry norms with a business card that is virtually indestructible.

Yes, the indestructible business card exists. But much better than your traditional business card that simply has your address, name and phone number, this business card does so much more—in fact, there is no limit to what you can do with this business card. You can educate and inform your prospective clients about your area of law, provide details about your wonderful professional background and show consumers why you are the perfect lawyer for their case. But even better, this business card gives you a virtual guarantee that it will never been thrown out and will remain with your clients and peers for years to come.

THE BEST BUSINESS CARD IN THE WORLD IS A BOOK

Before you start thinking, "This guy Fisher is nuts, why would I write a book?" you should ask one question, **When was the last time you threw out a book?** Okay, maybe you've donated some books to the local library or sold a few books at a garage sale, but I'm willing to bet you've never thrown out a book. But why?

Books are sacrosanct in our culture. And we're not talking about e-books—real, physical books you hold in your hands. And yes, even the books you've never read or maybe started reading but didn't like—all of these books hold a special place in our culture that says one thing: you better not toss me out! So, even though you don't like the clutter, the books (yes, even books you've never read) sit on your coffee table in your living room and stare you in the face day after day.

Perhaps you don't give a single thought to the book, but it still sits there. You have parties and friends over to the house, and that book is still sitting there for all to see. Endless people see the book over the course of years and it's got dust all over it, but it still sits there.

HOW YOU CAN USE A BOOK TO CHANGE YOUR PRACTICE

Let's say you have an elder law practice and you've written a treatise, guide or book about special needs trusts (just stick with me for a moment). You have a new prospective client, Mr. Jones, who wants to meet with you about a special needs trust for his brother and he is interviewing a number of elder law attorneys to find the best lawyer. So you meet with Mr. Jones, review the pros and cons of special needs trusts and at the end of your meeting, you hand him your book about special needs trusts.

Now you've got his attention. Mr. Jones has met with a number of elder law attorneys, but none of them have given him a book. With a surprised look on his face, Mr. Jones thinks, "What's this about?" So Mr. Jones goes home and begins reading and reads some more—he devours the information in your book because it reads as if it was written just for him. All of Mr. Jones's questions and concerns are answered in your book.

Before you handed your book to Mr. Jones, you were just another lawyer. After handing him your book, you are suddenly the lawyer who "wrote the book" and you are suddenly different from every other lawyer Mr. Jones has interviewed. Once he gets your powerful book that is chockfull of great information about special needs trusts, is there really any doubt whom Mr. Jones will hire for his attorney?

You are no longer competing with other lawyers for work—your book does all of the selling for you. Mr. Jones will be completely pre-sold on you as his lawyer because you gave him something that no other lawyer did—a book that is full of great information that answers all of his questions.

YOUR BOOK: A GIFT THAT KEEPS GIVING

But it gets even better. Your book about special needs trusts will sit on Mr. Jones's coffee table for the next ten or fifteen years and hey, maybe no one will read it, but who cares? By the time your book gets donated to the local library (remember, no one throws out books), your book will have been seen by hundreds of Mr. Jones's family and friends. And even when your case with Mr. Jones is long over, your book will be a constant reminder to him of the excellent work you did and he will refer you to his friends and family.

A book is a gift that keeps giving. Mr. Jones asks for more copies of your book to give to his friends and now you're in business. Your book is getting read by high quality prospects who you might actually want to represent (yes, the clients who can pay you). While you're sitting on a beach in the Caribbean, there are new prospective clients reading about you and how you can help them with their legal problem. New clients are presold on you before your first meeting with them and hey, why not, you're the lawyer who "wrote the book."

THE GREATEST LEAD GENERATION DEVICE ON THE PLANET

But we're just getting started. Rather than just keeping your book in a dusty bookshelf, you offer an electronic book to consumers on your website. In exchange for their name and address, you provide prospective clients with a free e-book that costs you nothing. While you're sleeping, new prospective clients are downloading your free e-book and devouring the information you give them. And yes, part of this is that they are reading about you and why you are the perfect lawyer for their case.

Maybe they don't have a case right now—maybe your prospective clients are just trolling for free information. But don't let that stop you. There's a reason why the consumer found your website and downloaded your free e-book—you are providing information that they need. And maybe they don't need your services right now, but there's at least a decent chance they will need you eventually and when the time is right, voila! You've got a new client.

Now you're growing your law firm beyond a regional practice. Prospective clients from outside your community are downloading your free e-book and calling you for representation. You're growing your law firm from a regional to a statewide and even national law practice and your book is the cornerstone building block for the growth of your firm. With a book, you're thinking of the future and building a system that will generate a steady pipeline of new clients and referrals that will keep your law firm open for years.

WHY ISN'T EVERYONE WRITING A BOOK?

Wait a minute, you say, how will you find time to write a book and even then, how will you find a traditional publishing house, like Harper-Collins or Simon-Schuster, to publish it? These are the type of thoughts that will stop you dead in your tracks.

If you set aside 30 minutes a day for writing, you can write a book in 3-6 months. Is it easy? No, but let's face it, nothing worth having is easy. And you won't need to do a load of research because the information you need to write your book is already in your head. You just need to sit down and start writing—no, not *War and Peace*, but just a couple of paragraphs a day. In just three or four weeks, you will be on your way with the first three chapters of your book. Believe me, you can do this.

Okay, but what about finding a publisher willing to publish your book? Don't let this stop you, my friend. There are self-publishing companies (I published my first book, *The Seven Deadly Mistakes of Malpractice Victims*, with self-publisher, Word Association) that can publish your book for $2,000 and yes, that includes proofreading, copy editing, graphic design of the front and back cover and interior layout. If you want to self-publish a book (and that's what

I recommend for your first book), a self-publishing company can publish your book in three months.

That's right, a book is the ultimate business card—an indestructible business building machine that you will have your entire career. Rather than keeping this information in your head, you give it all away in the book. And why, you ask, would you do this? It's simple: because no other lawyer in your town, county or maybe state has a book and when you're the lawyer who "wrote the book," you are creating a celebrity status that will set yourself apart from every other lawyer in your town.

24

A LESSON IN LIFE FROM A SHYSTER LAWYER

"Those who will succeed in the marketplace ... are the rule breakers, the noisemakers, the attention getters—the unreasonable ones. They are the 'untouchables' who regularly do things that set them apart from the economy as a whole."

—Grant Cardone, *If You're Not First, You're Last*

THIS WAS A LAWYER'S WORST NIGHTMARE.

One screw-up after the next ranging from missed court conferences to failing to file discovery responses in compliance with court-ordered deadlines, and even worse, having the case dismissed for failing to file a note of issue after being served with a 90-day demand. This New York City plaintiffs' law firm was having a really bad day—okay, maybe a bad couple of years.

To make matters even worse, the lawyers handling this medical malpractice case were less than truthful with the plaintiff. After the court dismissed the lawsuit for repeated failures to comply with court orders, the plaintiff's lawyers simply told their client that the lawsuit had no merit and should be voluntarily discontinued. Not knowing that the lawsuit had already been dismissed, the plaintiff signed a stipulation of discontinuance and the case was over.

Now, fast forward one year. The plaintiff discovers the truth about his lawsuit: his lawsuit was dismissed by the court, based upon the apparent incompetence of his lawyers and repeated acts of gross negligence. A legal malpractice lawsuit ensues against the plaintiff's former lawyers, and eventually, the case is settled for seven figures. (Just Google *Scarborough v. Napoli*, if you want more of the juicy facts about this case in Oswego County.) The plaintiff finally gets the justice he deserves.

Not the Lesson in Life You Expected

I know what you're thinking. The lesson from this case (you think) is that you should do your best to comply with court-ordered deadlines for discovery, file the note of issue when you're supposed to, and always be honest with your client. Well, not exactly, but yes, you should do those things.

It was difficult to comprehend how the shyster lawyer who was handling the legal malpractice suit was managing to practice law. Just one major screw-up after the next, and then, after two years of mind-numbing mistakes, the shyster lawyer attempted to hide the truth from his client (not a good idea). The depositions in the legal malpractice case offered no answers: the shyster lawyer was so unfamiliar with basic procedure in New York that it was difficult to accept that he had passed the bar exam.

But one thing came as an inexplicable surprise to everyone: the shyster lawyer had a past history of success with jury verdicts. Not just a little success but big verdicts in medical malpractice cases throughout New York—yes, the kind of results that any plaintiff's lawyer would be proud of. This was intriguing. Did the shyster lawyer simply have a single bad day in *Scarborough v. Napoli*? That seemed to be the case—until the truth was revealed.

A Shocking Discovery about the Shyster Lawyer

For perhaps no other reason than curiosity, I set out to discover how the shyster lawyer was so successful in getting great jury verdicts in other cases yet seemed so utterly incompetent in one lawsuit. So, I got the trial transcripts from several of the other lawsuits and set out to find out how this plaintiff's lawyer was somehow getting one fantastic jury verdict after the next. The answer was not what I expected.

The trial transcripts from the other lawsuits revealed one common theme: the shyster lawyer was thoroughly unprepared for just about every aspect of the trial, ranging from the direct examination of his key medical experts, cross-examination of the defense experts, and closing argument. As if that wasn't enough, the shyster lawyer did not have a basic grasp of the rules of evidence or New York's procedural laws. Yet, even with very difficult facts and facing the best defense lawyers in the state, the shyster lawyer was hitting home runs with one big jury verdict after the next.

Yes, the shyster lawyer was somehow moving from one courtroom to the next with tremendous results, even with little preparation and a tenuous grasp on the law. So, you ask, what is the valuable *lesson in life* from the shyster lawyer?

The Difference between Winners and Losers

Ninety-nine percent of plaintiffs' lawyers would never have accepted these cases and yet (call it blind luck if you want), the shyster lawyer racked up one jury verdict after the next. And, yes, luck was part of it, but if we stopped there, you would not be giving nearly enough credit to the shyster lawyer.

Rather than listen to the naysayers who told him that his cases sucked and he was sure to lose, the shyster lawyer disregarded their "advice" and just moved forward to trial. Yes, the shyster lawyer deserves credit that no one to this point would give him: *he took action.*

The shyster lawyer was facing down some of the preeminent defense lawyers in the state with cases that barely withstood defense motions for summary judgment. But rather than blaming the terrible facts of these cases and the long odds of winning (75 percent of malpractice trials are won by the defense, according to New York's Office of Court Administration, and the national rate of defense verdicts is even higher), the shyster lawyer threw caution to the wind and the results were stunning.

The Lesson for All of Us from the Shyster Lawyer

So, what does this mean for you? Take crappy cases, don't prepare for trial, and just hope for the best? Not quite. That is a roadmap for the destruction of your law career.

But let's face one brutal fact: in small-town America (and perhaps everywhere), the lawyers are keen on talking a big game. You hear the big talkers everywhere, but especially in bar rooms after they are primed for big talk with liquor and a receptive audience of other big-game talkers and dreamers. Yes, it's a sad fact that lawyers are full of hot air when it comes to talking, and 98 percent of the time, that's all it is: *talk.*

How many times have you heard other lawyers tell you that they're going to change their practice to become big-time "trial guys"? If you haven't heard this, just walk into a bar near a courtroom in your county and you're certain to overhear the big talkers at the bar. But the sad reality is that *it's just talk.*

Hockey legend Wayne Gretzky once said, "There is a 100 percent chance of missing a shot that you don't take." To his credit, the shyster lawyer adopted Wayne Gretzky's motto with the philosophy that you can't win a case that you don't take to trial.

The Shyster Lawyer Gets the Last Laugh

Back in the lawyers' lounge of the courthouse, there are few kind words for the shyster lawyer. The criticism is harsh and never-ending: "He's clueless," "He can't find his way around a courtroom to save his life," or perhaps, "He's just dumb lucky." And maybe the naysayers are right, but guess who's getting the last laugh?

The shyster's lawyer's bank account is fat. While the other lawyers are fighting for scraps, the shyster lawyer is laughing all the way to the bank. The shyster lawyer cares little about the criticism of his peers; he knows that his trial calendar is full for the next year and win or lose, he's going to be just fine.

"We reward for those who draw maps, not those who follow them."

—SETH GODIN, *Poke the Box*

The shyster lawyer is having his cake and eating it too by taking action and not worrying where the chips will fall. As the author Grant Cardone says, "The successful are willing to take gambles—to put it all out there and know, regardless of the outcome, that they can go back and do it again." (By the way, Grant Cardone's book *The 10X Rule* is an absolute must read).

But how will this lesson in life from the shyster lawyer help you?

How You Can Change Your Law Practice (and Your Life)—Right Now

But isn't it just easier to stay in your comfort zone and keep doing what you're doing? Hey, if you're happy where you are right now, there's no need to change a thing. But I'm guessing that's not quite the case if you're still reading.

"The cost of being wrong is less than the cost of doing nothing."

—SETH GODIN, *Poke the Box*

Here's my challenge for you: *Today* (not tomorrow or next week) take one simple action toward the achievement of your big audacious goal. It's okay if it's a small, baby step, but you have to take small steps toward the achievement of your goals *every day* and follow a daily discipline of taking another step tomorrow. Over time, the compounded impact of your daily actions will advance you slowly, but surely, toward your goals.

25

NUGGETS OF GOLD FOR YOUR SUCCESS AND SELF-IMPROVEMENT

"This is the single most powerful investment we can ever make in life—investment in ourselves."

—STEPHEN R. COVEY, *The 7 Habits of Highly Effective People*

WHY DO YOU COME TO WORK? Earn a few bucks and pay the grocery bills and mortgage? Of course, making money and paying the bills are important, but why are you really here?

I hired you for one reason: you are a *superstar*! That's right, you are the absolute best at what you do and you will be treated that way. You deserve to be treated as a superstar, but what does that mean?

You will have resources available to you that no other law firms offer their employees at no charge. But it will be up to you to take advantage of this opportunity for self-improvement and growth. I will not force self-improvement upon you. But if you're my kind of person (and if I hired you, you better be), my guess is self-improvement is your goal too.

Self-Improvement Seminars That Can Change Your Life

"Successful people dream big and have immense goals. They are not realistic. They leave that to the masses, who fight for the leftovers."

—GRANT CARDONE, *The 10X Rule*

Let's get started with the list of seminars and workshops available at no charge to you—yes, that means I'm footing the bill:

Dale Carnegie: Dale Carnegie is the premier self-improvement training in the world. If there's ever anything you thought impossible, Dale Carnegie will train you to tackle those challenges. Simply stated, Dale Carnegie is life-changing if you implement its principles.

So, what's stopping you? Take me up on this offer of free Dale Carnegie training and you will never look back … and your life will never be the same.

Great Legal Marketing: *Great Legal Marketing and its founder, Ben Glass, Esq., have changed my life.* If you get a chance to attend one of Ben's seminars, just go. Ben is the premier business development and marketing expert for lawyers in the country.

If you've ever dreamed of operating the best law firm, Ben will give you the blueprint and teach you how to get home in time for dinner with your family. I don't listen to anyone else—Ben is that good.

InfusionCon: There is no better small business marketing machine than Infusionsoft based in Chandler, Arizona. Infusionsoft is a world-class, small-business marketing company that presents an annual convention known as InfusionCon. The enthusiasm and spirit of those attending InfusionCon is off the charts.

Look, it doesn't hurt that the InfusionCon conventions are held in sunny Arizona in the late winter. So, just go and be amazed at the outside-the-box marketing and self-improvement skills you get from the leaders of InfusionCon.

Dan Kennedy: There is no marketing expert in the country who can hold a candle to Dan Kennedy. Read all of Dan's books. There is no better place to start.

If all you did was read Dan's books, you'd be just fine. The No BS series of books is chock-full of practical advice for anyone running a small business or law firm.

Why it's done this way: If you simply earn money for me and nothing else, I haven't done justice for you. My goal is to make you a better person through self-improvement seminars and workshops that are designed to not just make you a better employee but a more committed and dedicated spouse and parent.

"Training isn't a perk; it's a tremendous business advantage."

—JIM COLLINS, *Beyond Entrepreneurship*

All of our team members receive training from Dale Carnegie, Dave Ramsey (EntreLeadership), Infusionsoft (InfusionCon), and Ben Glass, Esq. (Great Legal Marketing) for *free*. So, it's up to you to take advantage of this great opportunity for growth and self-development.

But even if you don't want to attend these seminars, you have $5,000 in spending money every year to attend the seminars of your choice. The $5,000 in spending money for self-improvement seminars is part of the compensation package.

The A Team for Your Law Firm

Let's face it, you can't do this alone. You need help. Through a ton of trial and error, I've assembled an A Team of experts for all aspects of law office management and systems. So, don't recreate the wheel; hire this team of experts and you won't hire anyone else again.

Graphic design: Julee Hutchison, Hutchison-Frey, 5355 McKenzie Springs Road, Placerville, Colorado 81430 (970-327-4565):

Graphic designer extraordinaire and an amazing asset for any law practice, Julee does all of my monthly newsletters for my referral partners, *Lawyer Alert*, and graphic work for my trial lawyer workshop, "The Jury Project." I could not get it done without Julee. Consider yourself lucky if you get a chance to work with Julee.

Fulfillment and publishing: Help Without Hassle (Michelle Foster), 1492 Janasu Road, McPherson, Kansas 67460 (620-504-6217):

Michelle Foster is the best fulfillment provider in the business. Michelle can work with any deadline and has the attitude of "I'll get it done" for every new project. If you have time-sensitive deadlines for new projects, Michelle is the person for the job. BTW: Michelle and Julee Hutchison work very well together.

Audio and video support and courtroom exhibits: Litigraphics, LLC (Mark Whalen), 26 Sunset Terrace, Baldwinsville, New York (315-635-3653):

The best videographer and courtroom exhibit expert, Mark is just a tremendous asset for any trial lawyer and a great guy to boot. I use Mark in just about every trial, and he hasn't said no to a last-minute work project yet. If you give Mark a shot on one of your cases, you won't regret it.

Webmaster for lawyers: Foster Web Marketing (Tom Foster), 10555 Main Street, Suite 470A, Fairfax, Virginia 22030 (571-251-7386):

Simply the best webmaster for lawyers on the planet. If you want to get serious about internet marketing, you can do no better than Tom Foster and his great team.

Marketing for Lawyers: Great Legal Marketing (Ben Glass, Esq.), 3915 Old Lee Highway, Suite 22-B, Fairfax, Virginia 22310 (703-591-9829):

Ben Glass, Esq. is the *authority* on marketing and law office systems and office management. Ben has had a huge impact on my professional development (and truth be told, my life) and I know he can do the same for you.

The best thing you can do for your career is to attend Ben Glass, Esq.'s seminar, "Great Legal Marketing." Your head will explode with the great information that Ben provides.

Screening new case calls for lawyers: Legal Intake Professionals, 300 10th Avenue South, Nashville, Tennessee 37203 (615-263-5222):

Are you wasting your time with new case calls that are just garbage? Do you want to pick and choose the new clients who get to speak with you? Legal Intake Professionals has a team of professionals who will answer the new case calls for you and patch the new calls through to your office if the case has merit. Legal Intake Professionals can save you and your team a ton of time weeding through new case calls.

Phone service for lawyers: Call Ruby, 1331 NW Lovejoy Street, #875, Portland, Oregon 97209 (866-611-7829; www.callruby.com):

Call Ruby is not your ordinary call answering service. Without fail, Call Ruby will answer your phones with a big smile and an enthusiastic voice. Call Ruby will answer your phones, or any overflow of calls from your primary receptionist, for very reasonable fees. The service provided by Call Ruby is exceptional.

The person answering your phones is the face of your law firm. The problem is most receptionists can be cold and impersonal. Call Ruby is your answer.

Case software management: Trialworks, 1550 Madruga Avenue, Suite 508, Coral Gables, Florida 33146 (305-357-6500):

Simply the best case management software for a litigation law firms. Check out the competition and you'll find there are plenty of case management software companies but none like Trialworks for a litigation lawyer. Save yourself some time; just hire Trialworks.

Why it's done this way: Let's face it, you can't do this alone. You need a team. Through trial and error, I've created a tremendous team. You can feel free to contact any of members of my team to find out what they can do for you.

Nine Books That Are Essential Reading for Your Growth and Self-Improvement

What is the greatest skill a person can have? Is it the ability to dissect a hostile witness during cross-examination? No! Reading great works of literature is easily the most important skill that a lawyer or nonlawyer can have. But we're all too busy to read, right?

This is my top-nine list of the books that should be at the very top of your to-read list. These books are classic reads on the topic of self-improvement. Do yourself a big favor and *read at least ten pages a day*. It won't take long, and your life will be changed immeasurably.

THE SLIGHT EDGE BY JEFF OLSON

In his incredible book *The Slight Edge* Jeff Olson explains why 95 percent fail miserably to accomplish their goals in life and live a life of quiet desperation. Only one out of 20 persons will achieve his/her goals in life, but why?

Jeff Olson's formula for success: a few simple disciplines, repeated every day. As Olson writes, "It's simple to do, and simple not to do," but the compounded effect of simple disciplines followed every day will transform your life. But you will not see the results of your actions immediately. Success doesn't come overnight; it takes a lot of time and hard work.

Do one thing before you read on: buy *The Slight Edge*. This book has the power to change your life!

THE E-MYTH REVISITED BY MICHAEL E. GERBER

Ever wonder why over 80 percent of franchised businesses succeed while roughly 95 percent of nonfranchised businesses fail? Franchised businesses, such as McDonald's, have systems for every aspect of their business, while other businesses have no systems. Having systems for running a law firm is the secret to running a successful business.

If you let your employees decide how they will do things, they will choose their way of doing things. This haphazard "nonstrategy" of letting your employees decide how to do their work is a formula for failure. Instead, you create specific policies that govern every aspect of how your law firm is run. And as Michael E. Gerber says, "the more automatic the system is, the more effective your franchise prototype will be."

I wrote this book with exactly that goal in mind. I wanted to create systems that control every aspect of a personal injury law firm, not just for New York lawyers but for any lawyer with an injury law firm.

So, what are the "rules of the game" for your law firm? Today, you should create very specific rules for your law firm, just like those in this book, that govern every activity in your law firm from answering phones to requesting medical records.

THE 7 HABITS OF HIGHLY EFFECTIVE PEOPLE BY STEPHEN R. COVEY

The biggest flaw of almost all lawyers: getting caught doing the barrage of new things that get thrown at them every day. When you are simply reacting to new stuff, it's impossible to be productive.

But we all know that 20 percent of our cases bring 80 percent of our income (aka the Pareto principle). So, why do we ignore our best cases that will make most of our money? As Stephen R. Covey says, "Effective management is putting first things first." Putting first things first puts your "A" cases at the top of your to-do list and focuses on work that will sustain your law practice with business development and marketing.

Ask yourself, "What one thing could I do in my personal and professional life that, if I did on a regular basis, would make a tremendous positive difference in my life?" Now, try to focus your time only on this activity.

The 7 Habits of Highly Effective People is a must-read for anyone serious about self-improvement and should be read over and over again.

THE 10X RULE BY GRANT CARDONE

As the author says, "Winning is only possible with massive actions." It's simply not enough to have big dreams without massive action. Losers talk about grand dreams and plans, while winners just take action and make stuff happen without the fear of failure.

Massive action, more than anything else, separates the winners from the losers. Grant Cardone's philosophy of taking 10 times more action than your competitors, without the fear of failure or criticism from your peers, is a formula for success.

GOOD TO GREAT BY JIM COLLINS

Ever wonder what makes great leaders and profitable companies? Jim Collins answers this question with the hedgehog concept in *Good to Great*. The "hedgehogs" are the leaders and companies that stick to three guiding principles: they find out what they do better than anyone else; what they are deeply passionate about; and what drives their "economic engine" (i.e., profit).

Can your law firm succeed in a dire economy for lawyers? Guess which company in the S&P 500 had the highest rate of return for investors between 1970 and 2001? This company just happens to be in the worst possible industry imaginable. Yes, Southwest Airlines thrived in an industry that was beset by bankruptcies and failed mergers. If Southwest Airlines can thrive in the worst industry, there's nothing stopping you, as a lawyer, from doing the same in a business overflowing with competitors.

HOW TO STOP WORRYING AND START LIVING BY DALE CARNEGIE

How to Stop Worrying and Start Living is a life changer for anyone lucky enough to read this amazing book.

About 90 percent of the things in our life are good and only 10 percent are bad. In Dale Carnegie's immortal words, "if we want to be happy, all we have to do is concentrate on the 90 percent that are right and ignore the 10 percent that are wrong." Dale Carnegie's book is chock-full of interesting, real-life examples of people who overcame enormous obstacles involving severe injury and financial failure by refusing to focus on the negative, and instead, giving thanks for the blessings in their lives.

THE 4-HOUR WORKWEEK BY TIMOTHY FERRIS

The concept is a great one: you should be doing the work that *only you can do* and outsource everything else. Timothy Ferris talks about the 24/7 workplace where "it's a strange feeling having people work for you while you're asleep."

Now, I know what you're thinking: "This would never work in my profession." Au contraire, my friend. The goal is to "free your time to focus on bigger and better things" and that won't happen if you're doing the technical work of a law practice such as typing pleadings and discovery responses. And this doesn't just apply to your law firm; you should be delegating and assigning personal errands as mundane as grocery shopping and cooking dinner. Each time you are about to do something, ask yourself, "Could someone else do this?"

If Donald Trump has five administrative assistants, shouldn't you have at least one? You don't have to recreate the wheel to have a successful life; roadmaps from the ultrasuccessful are everywhere. Just start reading 10 pages a day of a success book, and you will be amazed at the long-term impact it will have on you personally and professionally.

NO B.S. RUTHLESS MANAGEMENT OF PEOPLE & PROFITS BY DAN KENNEDY

Just read any book written by Dan Kennedy, but if you could only read one, read this. Most business owners want to be well liked among their employees. Big mistake! Just like Bill Parcells, the Hall of Fame football coach who was disliked by most of his players, your only goal is to get results and make money.

As Dan says, "If you occasionally accept occasional unacceptable behavior, it's only a matter of time before you'll be routinely accepting unacceptable behavior." You have to be ruthless in enforcing the highly specific standards and systems that you set for your law firm. Otherwise, the inmates will be running the asylum.

The No BS series is must reading. If you read one of Dan's books, you won't stop until you're finished.

HOW TO WIN FRIENDS AND INFLUENCE PEOPLE BY DALE CARNEGIE

In law school you were taught concepts that show you how to do the technical aspects of the law. But the theory of the law is just a small part of the practice of law. Far more important is your ability to interact with others and see things from their point of view.

But it's a common mistake to think that Dale Carnegie is all about public speaking. Yes, part of Dale Carnegie training is public speaking, but it's really developing the courage to break through your comfort zones and do things that you never dreamed possible. If you take action and implement Dale Carnegie's principles, your life will be profoundly changed.

No book has had a bigger influence on my life than Dale Carnegie's *How to Win Friends and Influence People.* This timeless classic should be must reading in every college in America and every company should offer its employees free training through Dale Carnegie. If you are serious about the personal growth and development of your employees, you should offer Dale Carnegie training to your employees as part of their compensation package.

26

THREE SIMPLE
SECRETS TO SUCCESS

*"If you have no successful example to follow in whatever
endeavor you choose, you may simply look at what
everyone else around you is doing and do the opposite
because—THE MAJORITY IS ALWAYS WRONG."*

—EARL NIGHTINGALE, *Lead the Field*

YOU'VE MADE IT THIS FAR. You are studying success literature and you're out in the field running a law firm. The principles set forth in this book will help set you on a path for building the law firm of your dreams. But there's just one more thing—and without this one thing, you will struggle daily to build a law firm that surpasses all others.

The First Stage of Learning: Reading

"Poor people have big TVs. Rich people have big libraries."

—Jim Rohn

There are three stages to the learning process (for building a law practice and just about everything): *study, do, and mentor.*

To build a dynamic, growing law firm, you must continually study and read new books. I'm not talking about the latest Harry Potter book, *People* magazine, or for that matter, any fiction. Fiction will not help you at all. I'm talking about reading the finest success, nonfiction books, such as any of Dan Kennedy's books.

Without continual learning, you are just maintaining the status quo, and the status quo is not an option. As suggested by Jeff Olson in *The Slight Edge*, you only need to read 10 pages of a book once a day. Yes, that's all it takes. If you read just 10 pages a day from a book such as *The Slight Edge*, you will have read a dozen books by the end of the year. Just think how far ahead of the pack you'll be.

> *"It's not an accident that successful people read more books."*
>
> —Seth Godin, *Linchpin*

Reading just 10 pages from a new book will alone put you far above the pack of other lawyers who complain and moan about the unfairness of life. If you do this one thing *every day*, you'll have taken a huge step away from those lawyers (the 95 percent who fail) who are convinced that fate and circumstances beyond their control are the reason for their failure. As Mark Twain wrote, "The man who does not read good books has no advantage over the man who can't read them."

Why not start by reading the nine books listed in Chapter 25. I promise you that each book will open your eyes to a way of life that less than 5 percent of lawyers live. But even if you read just five pages of a new book every day, you will be way ahead of others at the end of the year because, let's face it, most people don't read at all.

But you should go a step further. Instead of listening to the radio during your drive to work every day, why not spend just 15 minutes listening to success books on audio CD or your mp3? Will this make a big difference in your life? After day one, you will see no results, and maybe after weeks or a month, you will see little difference in your attitudes and philosophy. But with just 15 minutes a day listening to success books on tape, you will see huge results by the end of the year.

To paraphrase Jeff Olson in *The Slight Edge*: simple disciplines, compounded daily, will change your life over time.

The Second Stage of Learning: Doing

> *"The successful are willing to take gambles—to put it all out there and know, regardless of the outcome, that they can go back and do it again."*
>
> —GRANT CARDONE, *The 10X Rule*

Simply reading without doing is useless.

But isn't there just a ton of stuff that you have to do? I don't want you to do everything. All you need to do is take one simple daily step every day and yes, it's easy to do and easy not to do. You may not notice any difference in your practice over the next week or the next month. But I promise you this: the compounded effect of simple daily steps taken every day will have a dramatic impact on your practice. In one or two years, you will be amazed at the results.

And here's a little bonus tip: DO ONE THING EVERY DAY THAT *YOU ARE SCARED TO DEATH OF DOING!* Yes, you know what I'm talking about—everyone has something that you're just putting off because it's outside of his or her comfort zone. But you're not the 99% of lawyers who live "quiet lives of desperation"— instead you live outside-the-box by forcing yourself to do things that you never dreamt were possible.

If there is just one thing that makes you sweat just thinking about it, perfect! Just do it. The worst that will happen is you will fail— who cares? Are you any worse off? Remember, failure is a learning opportunity on your road to the law firm of your dreams—but NOT TRYING will be catastrophic to your career.

> **"Refuse to live by the social norms of the mediocre."**
>
> —GRANT CARDONE, *If You're Not First, You're Last*

Once you get in the habit of living outside your comfort zone, you won't remember what your life was like before. Right now, write down two or three things that you are scared to death of. Okay, now you've got your roadmap for action. Remember, goals not written down and regularly reviewed are merely wishes.

The Third Stage of Learning: Mentor

> **"Those lucky enough to start with a supportive mentor and access to resources begin walking up the ladder and, with some pluck, can move quite high in the industrial pecking order."**
>
> —SETH GODIN, *The Icarus Deception*

Reading and doing is not enough.

Remember, your law firm is not a new experiment. Great law firms and businesses have been made before, so why not walk in the steps of those who have gone before you and learn from their mistakes and failures?

But this is the one thing that less than 1 percent of lawyers will ever do. *You need a mentor.* And yes, I don't care if you have 20 years of experience and you already know the basics of running a successful law firm. With a mentor, you will leverage the experiences and successes of other lawyers and benefit from their collective wisdom.

This is where 99.9 percent of lawyers fail. Call it pure ego and perhaps you want to stay in your comfort zone, but once you leverage the knowledge and wisdom of successful lawyers, you then have a roadmap for success. Instead of walking on landmines, you will have a successful lawyer walking you around the landmines that can ruin your law practice.

But I know what you're thinking: where will you find a top caliber lawyer willing to share his/her time with you? Napoleon Hill, author of the classic book *Think and Grow Rich*, calls this the *power of the mastermind*. Napoleon Hill introduced the concept of the mastermind group in the early 1900s as this: "The coordination of knowledge and effort of two or more people who work toward a definite purpose, in the spirit of harmony."

A mastermind group is a powerful way to leverage the experiences and knowledge of other lawyers who have discovered through trial and error the best way to run a successful law firm. Rather than recreate the wheel, you learn what has worked best for other lawyers so you don't make the same mistakes they made.

A mastermind group doesn't have to be limited to lawyers. You can invite small business owners from outside the law, perhaps a self-employed home inspector, to find out the steps they've taken to grow their businesses. But the idea of the mastermind group is to meet once a month with the group to discuss strategies to grow your law practice, keep yourselves accountable for your goals, and maximize profit.

A mastermind group can be just two lawyers who agree to get together once a month to discuss what they are doing to move forward in the areas of marketing, finance, and operations. There is nothing better you can do for your law practice.

Yes, you need to be a part of a mastermind group. This is the most powerful thing you can do to build the law firm of your dreams.

CONCLUSION

*"You are either going for your dreams
or giving up on your dreams."*

—Jeff Olson, *The Slight Edge*

THERE ARE NO SHORTCUTS. There is no magic wand that you can waive, and voila! You suddenly have a successful law firm and a beachfront home on South Beach. This book is 26 chapters to drive home one point: a successful law practice is a marathon (26 miles) that requires simple, little steps forward every day. The goal of most lawyers (and just about everyone) to get rich quick is a fantasy.

But there is a magical secret to success and it is simple, undeniable, and unchanging:

"That's what successful people do: simple things that are easy to do. Here's the problem: every action that is easy to do is also easy not to do. If you don't do them, you won't suffer, or fail or blow it—today. But that simple error in judgment, compounded over time, will ruin your chances of success."

—Jeff Olson, *The Slight Edge*

And yes, that's all it takes, simple little actions, repeated over time, that have the compounded effect of changing your life. And it all starts with a single step forward every day. Yes, a simple discipline of action that is "easy to do, and easy not to do."

All that's required is taking the first step. The past is irrelevant; the only thing that matters is *now*. But there's no more waiting for you. Perhaps it's just spending five minutes on the elliptical tonight or reading a book to your kids. But whatever it is, just get started.

Fate and circumstance will not decide your future. The future is in your hands. What will you do *today* that will contribute to your success?

A SPECIAL OFFER
FOR YOU

LET'S SAY YOU'RE JUST OPENING your new law firm. You have big dreams and goals and you can't wait to get started. But there's just one problem: you don't have any of the forms that you need for a successful injury law practice. And you sure don't want to recreate the proverbial wheel by drafting new forms, one at a time. So, what can you do?

There's a special gift waiting for you.

Over the course of my 21-year career, I've found that it didn't make sense to create new documents every time I had to draft a motion, pleading, expert response, or discovery demand. So, I saved many of the best forms that I created. The forms range from interrogatories in a tractor trailer accident case to unique Arons authorizations that are tailored to make sure the defense lawyer doesn't become best friends with the treating physicians. Just about every form you will ever need to run a successful law firm.

The forms are indexed and categorized so you can easily identify the form that you need. These forms are contained in a flash drive and are easy to access from any computer. *And they are my special gift to you.*

You can get the flash drive simply by asking for it on the home page of my website, www.ultimateinjurylaw.com, or just give me a call at 1-866-889-6882, or e-mail at jfisher@fishermalpracticelaw.com to request the flash drive, and my trusted paralegal will mail the flash drive to you right away.

But wait, there's another gift for you.

I have a monthly newsletter for lawyers, *Lawyer Alert*, that provides tips about law office systems, management and practice. *Lawyer Alert* will keep you updated on changes in the law and unique practice management tips for injury lawyers.

"I keep all of your newsletters and I suspect a lot of other attorneys do also."

—PATRICK J. HIGGINS, ESQ., Powers & Santola, LLP, Albany, New York

I usually only mail *Lawyer Alert* to the attorneys on my A list—mostly lawyers who refer new cases. But if you send me an e-mail or call my office to request the newsletter, you'll receive *Lawyer Alert* near the first of every month for free. No strings attached!

But there's just one thing I'll ask.

If you have a malpractice or catastrophic injury case in New York, and you're looking to refer the case, give me a call. My practice is entirely based on lawyer referrals from people just like you, and I offer generous referral fees, and your rights to a referral fee will be protected in writing from day one. But even if you don't refer a single case to me, you'll still get *Lawyer Alert* every month and the flash drive.

Don't hesitate to call me at 1-866-889-6882 if you want to discuss a new case or just talk strategy for one of your upcoming trials.

ABOUT JOHN

JOHN FISHER is AV rated with Martindale-Hubbell, selected as a *Super Lawyer* by Thomson-Reuters, and has a perfect 10/10 rating from www.avvo.com. John is a graduate of the University of Notre Dame and Notre Dame Law School (and a huge fan of the Fighting Irish and Chicago Bears). John was a partner at Powers & Santola, LLP in Albany between 1996 and 2010, and for the last 17 years, John's practice has been limited to the representation of catastrophically injured persons.

John was awarded the Marketer of the Year by Great Legal Marketing in 2013 and has been called a "master at referral marketing" by Ben Glass, Esq., the nation's leading authority on marketing for lawyers.

John lives in Ravena, New York, with his three beautiful kids, Liliya, Tim, and Alek, and his lovely and talented wife (another lawyer), Lisa, and in his free time, he loves to slalom and barefoot waterski.

John is the author of the book, *The Seven Deadly Mistakes of Malpractice Victims*, which he offers free to injury victims everywhere. John's website, www.protectingpatientrights.com, is a treasure trove of information for victims of medical malpractice and is updated daily with new content on his blog, frequently asked questions, and articles.

John publishes a monthly newsletter just for lawyers, *Lawyer Alert*, that is mailed on the twenty-sixth day of every month to lawyers. *Lawyer Alert* provides tips about law office systems, management, and practice that you will not find anywhere else.

John has a podcast on iTunes, *The Ultimate Practice Builder for New York Injury Lawyers*, where he interviews experts on issues ranging from Medicare set-aside trusts, mobile websites, automated marketing, and lien resolution. You can download the podcast for free on iTunes.

You can get started building the injury law practice of your dreams by going to John's website, www.ultimateinjurylaw.com. This website was built just for YOU, injury lawyers trying to build better practices and get home in time for dinner with your family. Ultimateinjurylaw.com is full of great information about law office systems, practice and management that you won't find anywhere else. Check it out!

John's Twitter handle is www.twitter.com/JFisherLawyer and his Facebook page is www.facebook.com/protecting.patient.rights. John posts new content on Twitter, Facebook, and Google Plus every day.

John has been cited as a legal expert by the *New York Law Journal* and he speaks frequently to bar associations and trial lawyer organizations. John's workshop, "The Jury Project," educates lawyers how to use focus groups to prepare for their next trial, and his PowerPoint speech "How to get your Law Firm's Website on the First Page of Google" outlines the most common mistakes that lawyers make with internet marketing and what you can do today to start getting cases from your website. John provides free CLE credits for you or your organization and picks up the tab for dinner/lunch.

John is always more than willing to speak to any lawyer organization that would like a free CLE presentation on focus groups ("The Jury Project") or Internet marketing. To book a speaking engagement with John, please call 866-889-6882 to request a date.

Don't be bashful.

John is interested in your success, and welcomes your calls or e-mails. If you have questions or challenges creating systems for the technical, managerial, or entrepreneurial aspects of your law firm, please contact John at 1-866-889-6882 or e-mail him at jfisher@ fishermalpracticelaw.com.